# ISLĀMIC *TAHDHĪB*
# *AKHLĀQ*:
## Theory and Practice

Junior Level - General

B. AISHA LEMU

Iqra' International Educational Foundation, Chicago

# Part of a Comprehensive and Systematic Program of Islamic Studies

**A Textbook in IQRA Program of Islamic Akhlaq Junior Level / General**

**Islamic Tahdhib and Akhlaq**

**Chief Program Editors**
Dr. Abidullah al-Ansari Ghazi
(Ph.D., History of Religion
Harvard University)

Tasneema Khatoon Ghazi
(Ph.D., Curriculum-Reading
University of Minnesota)

**Religious Review**
Maulana Shu'aib ud-Din Qutub
(Faḍil Dar ul-Ulum, Karachi)

Najiyah Helwani

**Language Editing**
Hina Naseem
(B.S. Zoology, University of Maryland
M.A. (National Lewis University)

Huda Quraishi-Ahmed
(B.S., University of Illinois, Chicago)

**English Typesetting**
Shaista N. Ali
(M.A. Mass Communications, Karachi
University, Pakistan)

**Designer**
Kathryn Heimberger
(A.A.S. American Academy of Art)

**Production coordinator:**
Aliuddin Khaja

**Cover Art**
Seema Khan

Copyright © June 1997, IQRA' International Educational Foundation. All Rights Reserved.

Fifth Printing June, 2007
Proudly Printed in The U.S.A

**Special note on copyright:**
This book is a part of IQRA's Comprehensive and Systematic Program of Islamic Education.

No part of this book may be reproduced by any means including photocopying, electronic, mechanical, recording, or otherwise without the written consent of the publisher. In specific cases, permission is granted on written request to publish or translate IQRA's works.  For information regarding permission, write to:
**IQRA  International Educational Foundation,
7450 Skokie Blvd., Skokie, IL  60077
Tel: 847-673-4072
Fax : 847-673-4095**

Library of Congress Catalog Card Number 97-71699
ISBN # 1-56316-320-9

# TABLE OF CONTENTS

## I. ISLĀMIC *TAHDHĪB* AND *AKHLĀQ*: The Theory

## II. ISLĀMIC *TAHDHĪB* AND *AKHLĀQ*: The Practice

# IQRA´s NOTE: To Teachers and Parents

IQRA' International Educational Foundation is pleased to publish the revised edition of Sister B. Aisha Lemu's book, *Tahdhīb* and *Sīrah* as Islāmic *Tahdhīb* and *Akhlāq*: *Theory and Practice*. This textbook was written as part of the Islāmic Studies Curriculum for the Nigerian school system in 1983. Published at a time when Islāmic literature for children was scarcely available, Sister Lemu's series of textbooks was truly a pioneering effort in the field of Islāmic Studies. Subsequently, many of these books found their way to educational institutions throughout Western Europe and America.

The subject of moral education, *Tahdhīb* and *Akhlāq*, is considered vital in Islam and covers a broad range of topics. While moral education is obviously important for individual development, it also defines the character of the entire society. The Qur'ān and *Hadīth*, our richest resources for moral education, cover almost every aspect of life in both specific and general terms. By describing the moral and ethical struggles of the early prophets and their followers, The Qur'ān and *Hadīth* provide detailed accounts of the benefits of moral living. By contrast, the consequences of amorality are illustrated by the ill fate of those who rejected true faith. Moreover, the *Sīrah* of Prophet Muhammad ﷺ, provides the most perfect practical example of both theory and practice. Islāmic history provides many other practical examples of Islāmic *Akhlāq* and *Tahdhīb* through the lives of the *Sahābah* and other pious Muslims.

Unfortunately, much of this moral education does not reach our children for two reasons: (a) they cannot read the Arabic books and (b) the complete translated Qur'ān and volumes of *Hadīth* are too advanced for their level of reading. The study of a few selected verses from the Qur'ān and selected *Ahadīth* cannot adequately cover the subject of moral education in a systematic manner.

In this textbook, a broad spectrum of moral and social teachings and important biographies are covered in a systematic and organized fashion giving both the theory and practical examples in real life of Islāmic *Akhlāq* and *Tahdhīb*. The textbook uses Qur'ānic verses and carefully authenticated *Aḥadīth* as a basis for the lesson. Students should try to memorize these verses and *Aḥadīth* and their English translation.

The revised edition is divided into two parts. The first part is a textbook based on the teachings of Islāmic *Tahdhīb* and *Akhlāq*, organized in graded lessons for classroom or home-schooling purposes. The second part is an enrichment section, providing practical models of Islāmic virtues using biographical sketches of the prophets, *Ṣaḥābah*, and other pious Muslims. In addition, the new revised version has the following characteristics:

- It has been revised to include the issues relevant to Muslim communities in the West and the social environment they are living in.
- Recognizing the fact that there is now growing interest in the systematic study of Islam among Muslims and non-Muslims (to which persons like Sister Lemu have contributed creatively, *Al-hamdu li Allāh* ﷻ) and important material has been produced in all the areas of Islāmic Studies, many parts of the text have been rewritten.
- Sources of references to the Qur'ān and *Ḥadīth*, which were missing in earlier editions, are now provided accurately.
- The Qur'ānic text has been added. Both teacher and student can follow those sections of the Qur'ān relevant to the theme of the lesson.
- Important material from the Qur'ān and *Ḥadīth* has been added to elaborate certain subjects for better understanding.
- Islāmic terminology is used instead of English terminology.
- Islāmic invocations are added in place of English letters.
- Transliteration marks are placed on all Arabic letters.
- Important concepts are recapped in the WE HAVE

viii

LEARNED section and reinforced by EXERCISES at the end of each section.

- The quality of production and graphics has been improved.
- Readability tests apply to junior level according to the American school system; the teachers in other countries and regions will have to use their own judgment in recommending and using this book.

This revised edition is currently being presented for further review and field-testing. It is IQRA's policy to continue to improve the quality of published IQRA' material based on the reviews and comments we receive. We request all teachers, parents and readers to write to us their opinions on this book or other IQRA' material.

Chief editors,                                          Friday, 7 March 1997
7450 Skokie Boulevard, Skokie, IL.  60077     1417 *Jum'ah, Shawwal*

    Tel: 847-673-4072                              Fax: 847-673-4095

# Preface to the Original Edition

In writing this textbook, I have taken a fresh approach to Islāmic Studies. In the past, the tendency had been to teach Islam in terms of a set of traditional formulas to be memorized: the Articles of Belief, the Five Pillars, the Compulsory Acts of Ablution, etc. While these are essential aspects of Islāmic education, mere memorization of such facts does not instill enduring belief within the student. Living in a rational society, where Islam has to compete with many ideas and ideologies, we cannot expect to illuminate the questioning minds of our youth without offering the rationale behind these concepts.

Islam is the religion of *Fitrah* (the natural way). The Qur'ān itself is full of rational argument, thereby bringing the listener to a state of Iman (belief). The *Sīrah* of Rasulūllāh ﷺ itself guides us to both rational and practical aspects of life. It is our duty to present children with the information that will help them find solutions to their problems within the realm of Islam.

Our failure to accomplish this goal in the past has resulted in a vast number of marginal Muslims among the adult population. They are Muslims by birth and sentiment, but they have little or no knowledge of the true teachings of Islam. Islāmic morality and social standard are either unknown to most secular Muslims or disregarded as inconvenient or irrelevant.

If the growing child's spirit and intellect experience such an awakening, the search for better practice and further knowledge of Islam will follow automatically. But if we fail to awaken that Islāmic spirit *(Rūh al-Islām)* in the child, then no matter how many school examinations he passes, he will remain only a marginal Muslim, lacking the motivation to live, think and act as a Muslim.

The teacher is advised to bear this in mind when using this series. The Islāmic Studies lesson should be a period of challenge, mental exercise, communication and interaction between teacher and students. If it is a period of boredom, mental rest and endless repetition, the teacher is seriously at fault, and is taking the first steps towards rearing a new generation of marginal Muslims.

For detailed discussion of teaching methods, the teacher is referred to the author's earlier book: *Methodology of Primary Islāmic Studies - A Handbook for Teachers,* published by Islāmic Publications Bureau, P. M. B. 81, Lagos, Nigeria

I would like to thank my husband, Sheikh Ahmed Lemu, Grand *Qādi* of the <u>Shari'ah</u> Court of Appeal, Niger State, for checking the manuscripts and offering much useful advice. I am also grateful to IQRA' International educational Foundation for adopting this textbook in their comprehensive program of Islāmic Studies and revising it for American and Western audience.

B. Aisha Lemu
Mina, Nigeria

# ISLĀMIC *TAHDHĪB* **AND** *AKHLĀQ*

## Part I: Theory

# LESSON 1

---

## *TAHDHĪB* AND *AKHLĀQ*: MORAL EDUCATION

### What is *Tahdhīb* and *Akhlāq*?

*Tahdhīb* is derived from Arabic root word *Hadhaba*. *Hadhaba* means to train, clean, improve and refine someone. Thus, *Tahdhīb* means training and education for personal improvement and refinement. In other words, *Tahdhīb* means moral education. A moral is a standard of good behavior. Honesty, kindness, helpfulness, modesty, truthfulness are all examples of morals.

Another word that we use for morals and manners is *Akhlāq*. *Akhlāq* is derived from Arabic word *Khalaqa*. *Khalaqa* means to create, shape and mould. *Akhlāq* thus means naturally good temper, noble character and good manners. Islam teaches us:

> *All people are born on Fitrah, true noble nature.*
> (Transmitted by Bukhāri)

Environment can make one good or bad. The Qur'ān and the Sunnah teach us good morals and manners. Rasulūllāh ﷺ was the best example of the teachings of the Qur'ān. It is very important for a Muslim to learn about Islāmic *Tahdhīb* and *Akhlāq* and follow the Sunnah as the best model.

### What is the Need for *Tahdhīb* and *Akhlāq*?

Good moral behavior is the basis of a successful Islāmic life. Remember, life on earth began as a test from Allāh ﷻ to see if we would be His true servants and fight off the temptations of the *Shaiṭān*. On the Day of

1

Judgment, every human being will be asked how he or she behaved on earth. Those who obeyed Allāh ﷻ and exercised good moral judgment will be rewarded with eternal happiness in Paradise. Those who disobeyed Allāh ﷻ and sacrificed their morals for worldly gains will be punished with eternal unhappiness in Hell. Therefore, in order to please Allāh ﷻ and enter Paradise on the Day of Judgment, we must learn proper Islāmic *Tahdhīb* and practice *Akhlāq*.

In addition to making us successful in the afterlife, exercising proper *Tahdhīb* can also make our life here on earth more comfortable. If we are polite and treat people with respect, we gain their respect in return. If all human beings learn to respect each other, our lives will be peaceful and happy.

## How Do We Know the Difference Between Good and Bad?

We can recognize good actions from bad actions by looking at their results. For example, when you help someone, you know you have done a good deed, and you feel good about yourself. On the contrary, if you hurt someone, you know you have done something wrong; you've made him feel bad, so you don't feel good about yourself. As you can see, our own feelings show us the difference between right and wrong. In the Qur'ān, we are told that such feelings come from our conscience as Guidance from Allāh ﷻ.

Sometimes, it is hard to follow our conscience, because *Shaitān* tries to mislead us. When one feels confused, he should immediately refer to the Qur'ān and the Sunnah, which clearly define good Islāmic behavior and actions prohibited by Allāh ﷻ. The Qur'ān also gives the outcomes of such behavior, whether it is reward for good or punishment for bad. A good Muslim will be happy to do anything to please Allāh ﷻ. He will feel ashamed to do anything Allāh ﷻ prohibits.

Prophet Muhammad ﷺ was the best example of perfect behavior. His Companions (*Ṣahābah*) paid close attention to everything Rasulūllāh ﷺ said and did. Their reports were later written down and are known as *Ḥadīth*, traditions of the Prophet ﷺ. Rasulūllāh ﷺ's way of life and behavior were called his Sunnah. The Qur'ān says of the Prophet Muhammad ﷺ:

لَّقَدْ كَانَ لَكُمْ فِى رَسُولِ ٱللَّهِ أُسْوَةٌ حَسَنَةٌ لِّمَن كَانَ يَرْجُواْ ٱللَّهَ وَٱلْيَوْمَ ٱلْأَخِرَ وَذَكَرَ ٱللَّهَ كَثِيرًا ۝

*You have indeed in the Messenger of Allāh an excellent*
*example for those who hopes in Allāh*
*and the Final Day, and who remember Allāh much.*
(*Al-Ahzab* 33:21)

Rasulūllāh ﷺ reminded his followers before he died:

*I am leaving you with two things:  the Qur'an and my Sunnah:*
*whoever holds tight to them will never go astray.*
(Transmitted by Tirmidhi)

## Studying the Qur'an and Hadith

Every Muslim should study the Qur'ān and it's meaning to learn what Allāh ﷻ expects from us.  Every Muslim should also study the *Ḥadīth* and Sunnah to learn from Rasulūllāh ﷺ's example and follow his habits.  This is the only way we can learn best Islāmic *Akhlāq* and train ourselves in true Islāmic *Tahdhīb*.  It is important that every boy and girl learn these good habits early in life, because bad habits get harder to change as we get older.

By living a moral life, we can be an example for our fellow Muslims and non-Muslims.  Similarly, we can learn from the examples of our

3

good brothers and sisters. Even non-Muslims may be inspired by the righteous way of life Islam teaches. There are many misunderstandings among the non-Muslims about the Muslims. Islāmic *Tahdhīb* can be considered best form of Da'wah (invitation to Islam).

Every Muslim who tries to obey the teachings of the Qur'ān and the Sunnah of Rasulūllāh ﷺ will be guided and protected by Allāh ﷻ. He will travel safely on the Right Path *(as-Sirat al-Mustaqim)*. The rewards of his journey will be unlimited in the Hereafter.

## WE HAVE LEARNED:

* *Tahdhīb* is moral education.
* Good moral behavior is a major part of being a good Muslim.
* Allāh ﷻ and Rasulūllāh ﷺ have taught us the best manners to follow.

## EXERCISES

1. What does *Tahdhīb* mean?
2. What does *Tahdhīb* teach us?
3. What will every human being be asked about on the Day of Judgment?
4. In which book can we find Allāh's teachings about what is good and what is bad?
5. Which human being set the best example of good behavior?
6. What does Sunnah mean?
7. What does *Ḥadīth* mean?
8. Why is *Tahdhīb* very important for every Muslim boy and girl?

# LESSON 2

---

## OBEDIENCE TO PARENTS

### The Importance of Obedience to Parents

After obedience to Allāh ﷻ and His Messenger , it is most important to be obedient to one's parents. Being polite and helpful to one's parents is the duty of every Muslim.

Children sometimes do not realize how much their parents have done for them. Every mother bears the pains of pregnancy and childbirth. She often spends many sleepless nights patiently caring for her baby's needs. If the baby is sick, parents nurse him to health. They gladly spend their money and time to buy clothes, food and medicine for the baby and toys to make him happy.

As their child grows, they try to provide him a good education and a loving home. They are there for all the important events in their child's life, from his first words to his college graduation, professional career and marriage, giving him all their love and support. Even if he makes a mistake, they never stop loving him. Most of all, they pray that their child will grow up to be successful and happy in this life and in the Hereafter.

### Returning the Love and Kindness of Parents

Parents feel very happy if their son or daughter is kind, polite, helpful and obedient. If their child is rude, disobedient or lazy, they feel disappointed and even embarrassed.   After all, the way a child behaves reflects on his parents.

 When they become old and too weak physically to care for themselves, parents need loving care, just as they gave their children when they were young.  We should never forget that if our parents had not taken care of us when we were young and helpless, we probably would not have survived.  We truly owe our lives to our parents, so taking care of them in their old age should be our pleasure.

The Qur'ān commands us to show kindness to parents in the following words:

وَقَضَىٰ رَبُّكَ أَلَّا تَعْبُدُوٓاْ إِلَّآ إِيَّاهُ وَبِٱلْوَٰلِدَيْنِ إِحْسَـٰنًا إِمَّا يَبْلُغَنَّ عِندَكَ ٱلْكِبَرَ أَحَدُهُمَآ أَوْ كِلَاهُمَا فَلَا تَقُل لَّهُمَآ أُفٍّ وَلَا تَنْهَرْهُمَا وَقُل لَّهُمَا قَوْلًا كَرِيمًا ۝ وَٱخْفِضْ لَهُمَا جَنَاحَ ٱلذُّلِّ مِنَ ٱلرَّحْمَةِ وَقُل رَّبِّ ٱرْحَمْهُمَا كَمَا رَبَّيَانِى صَغِيرًا ۝

*Your Lord has decreed that you worship nothing but Him,*
*and that you be kind to parents. Whether one or both of them attain*
*old age in your life, say not to them a word of contempt, nor repel*
*them but address them in terms of honor.  And, out of kindness,*
*lower to them your wing of humility, and  say:  My Lord!*
*Bestow on them Your Mercy, even as they cherished me in childhood.*
*(Al-Isra' 17:23-4)*

6

# Obedience to Allāh ﷻ Comes First

If parents ask their children to do something which Allāh ﷻ has forbidden, children should obey Allāh ﷻ over the order of their parents. However, they should respectfully explain to their parents the reasons for their disobedience. If the parents are not Muslims, Rasulūllāh ﷺ taught us to be kind and respectful to them. We should take care of them and continue to explain Islam to them.

# How to Be Obedient and Helpful to Parents

In every home, many chores need to be done. When a child comes home from school, he should make it a point to help his parents before going off to play. Tidying up, washing clothes, mowing the lawn are a few ways we can help our parents. By offering our help, we show them how much we love and respect them.

Children should do their best to obey their parents. Children should not argue with their parents, refuse to help them, or make a fuss over every small matter. If a child is asked to take a bath, change clothes, do the vacuuming, or do homework, he/she should try to do so as soon as possible. Respecting our parents' wishes is another way we can show our parents we love them.

## WE HAVE LEARNED:

* Obedience to our parents is very important in Islam.
* We must be polite and loving to our mother and father.
* We should help our parents in jobs around the house.

## EXERCISES

1. A child should be _____ and _____ to his parents. (Fill in the blanks.)
2. What sorts of sacrifices do parents make for their children when they are young?
3. When parents grow old, why do they need special care from their children? What does the Qur'ān say about the care of parents when they are old?
4. Is there any occasion when a child should not obey his parents?
5. Give some other examples of helpfulness and obedience in daily life.

# LESSON 3

---

## CLEANLINESS

Cleanliness is a very important part of being a Muslim. Maintaining good personal hygiene shows respect for oneself and for those with whom one associates. The way a Muslim presents himself is a reflection on all Muslims and Islāmic teachings. This is why one should try to keep good habits of cleanliness.

Allāh ﷻ says to Rasulūllāh ﷺ:

*And your garments keep free from stain! And all abominations shun!*
*(Al-Muddathir 74:4-5)*

Rasulūllāh ﷺ is reported to have said:

> *(The religion of) Islam is clean. Hence, you should also keep*
> *yourself clean. No one will be allowed to enter Paradise except*
> *he who is clean. This cleanliness is of both the body and the mind.*
> (Transmitted by Bukhāri)

## Why is it Good to be Clean?

A dirty body, dirty hair, dirty teeth, and dirty clothes are not only unpleasant to look at, but give off a bad smell. They offend other people. They attract lice and disease-causing viruses. The dirty person may scratch his body that may cause sores resulting in infection. Dirty teeth become yellow

9

and rotten, causing pain.  They may even have to be pulled out.  But, clean, white teeth and a clean body in fresh, clean clothes are beautiful.  They are pleasant to experience and behold.

In the same way, if a person's mind and heart are clean, his character is good and pleasing. But if his mind is unclean, it is a place of bad thoughts and a source of bad deeds.

## How Should a Muslim Keep Himself Clean?

**The body:** A Muslim should try to bathe daily, if water is available.  It is an obligation to take a bath after wet dream or intimacy with one's wife.

**The hair:** The hair should be washed when bathing, whenever possible. The hair should always be combed and brushed.  Hair oil may be used.

**The teeth:**  The teeth should be brushed several times a day with a tooth-brush or a Miswak. It is recommended to brush the teeth at the time of Wudu. To brush teeth with a Miswak at the time of Wudu is a Sunnah of Rasulūllāh ﷺ.

Aishah ﵂, Rasulūllāh's wife, reported that he said:

> *The Miswak (tooth stick) is a means of purifying the mouth,*
> *and is pleasing to the Lord.*
> (Transmitted by Bukhāri)

The mind: A Muslim should have a clean mind and pure heart.  He should follow the guidance of the Qur'ān and the Sunnah. He should do what is good and avoid what Allāh ﷻ has forbidden.  If a Muslim does something wrong, he should immediately repent and try not to repeat his sin.  Regular prayers and fasting also help a Muslim to remember Allāh ﷻ and cleanse the heart and mind.

## Cleanliness for Salah

A Muslim should be particularly clean and nicely dressed for the *Salah*. He is about to stand before Allāh ﷻ, the Almighty, and must present himself in the best way possible. Therefore, cleansing oneself through *Wudu* or *Ghusl,* making sure that the clothes are clean and neat, and clearing the mind of bad thoughts are all parts of necessary purification in preparation for *Salah*.

## Cleanliness of Surroundings

A person cannot stay clean if he lives in a dirty environment. Therefore, a Muslim should keep his room, his house, his neighborhood and his environment clean. He should dispose of his garbage according to the city or neighborhood code. He should not leave it to blow around on other people's property or on the road. He should not use roads or sidewalks or public places to through waste or garbage. Following these teachings shows respect for Allāh ﷻ, respect for our neighbors, respect for the regulations of the society and respect for ourselves.

Keeping the environment clean keeps everyone healthy and happy. If we respect nature, it will respect us and continue to provide us our basic necessities, such as fruits, grains, wood, etc. However, if we abuse nature, we will lose all the benefits it provides us. All living things, whether human beings, plants, or animals, are the creation of Allāh ﷻ, and as good Muslims, we must respect all of Allāh ﷻ's creation.

## WE HAVE LEARNED:

* Cleanliness is part of our Iman (Faith).
* Our bodies should be clean to keep away sickness and disease.

11

\* We must keep all of our surroundings clean all the time.

## EXERCISES

1. What did Rasulūllāh  say about keeping clean?
2. What is the harm of a dirty body, hair, teeth and mind?
3. How should a Muslim clean his:
   (a) body?
   (b) hair?
   (c) teeth?
   (d) mind?
4. Why should a Muslim be clean and neat for prayers?
5. A Muslim should clean the place where he lives and his surroundings. Name two bad habits that he should avoid which may annoy other people.
6. What steps do you take to keep yourself and your clothes clean from the time you get up until the time you go to bed?

# LESSON 4

---

## RESPECT FOR ELDERS, TEACHERS AND AUTHORITY FIGURES

### A Muslim Shows Respect for His Elders

One of the best resources a child can have is the wisdom of his elders. Our elders have more knowledge of life than we do, because they have lived longer and have seen more of life than we have. We can learn a great deal from them. A good Muslim respects the wisdom of his elders by being polite and considerate to them. In return, his elders will be pleased with him and treat him kindly.

Anas 🌹 reported that Rasulūllāh 🕌 said:

> *No youth will honor an old man without Allāh*
> *appointing one to honor him when he is old.*
> (Transmitted by Tirmidhi)

Rasulūllāh 🕌 also informed us:

> *He who does not respect his elders and does not show*
> *love for the young ones is not from amongst us.*
> (Transmitted by Abu Da'wud)

### A Muslim Shows Respect for His Teachers

A Muslim youth should show respect for his teachers, whether they are

Muslims or non-Muslims, for the same reasons that he should respect all his elders. In addition, he should realize that his teacher is there to guide his behavior and his studies. The teacher helps him to become a better human being and earn a good living in the future.

Allāh ﷻ sent Rasulūllāh ﷺ as a teacher for us. Rasulūllāh ﷺ said:

> *Indeed, I have been sent as a teacher.*
> (Transmitted by Darimi)

Rasulūllāh ﷺ was a model teacher, and his are the best teachings. Teaching is a very important responsibility. A teacher cares very much about the progress of his students and tries to be patient with their mistakes. Therefore, a Muslim youth should be as cooperative as possible with his teacher. The teacher will be pleased with anyone who is polite and respectful.

## A Muslim Obeys Lawful Authority

Every social group has leaders: presidents, kings, judges, governors, mayors, principals, teachers and so on. These people have been appointed as the legal authorities in their areas or institutions. Their goal should be to work toward the greatest good for the group they lead.

People should participate in the political and social process. If they are living in a democratic society, they should take interest in elections and vote regularly. They should also offer advice to their leaders. They must respect the rules and regulations of the society. They must follow their leaders in all just causes. When people work together through a system of *Shura* (Consultation), they can achieve important things for the entire society. If people refuse to cooperate or remain indifferent, nobody can benefit.

For example, if someone wants to build a house, he appoints a contractor to direct the work. If the carpenters, masons, electricians and plumbers cooperate with him, they will soon make a fine house. But, if each worker ignores the foreman and does as he likes, the house may not be completed at all.

Therefore, a Muslim should cooperate with his leaders and obey them in all that is lawful. But, if they rule him to do what is unlawful and against the teachings of Islam, he should not obey. Obedience to Allāh ﷻ always comes first.

The Qur'ān says:

$$يَـٰٓأَيُّهَا ٱلَّذِينَ ءَامَنُوٓاْ أَطِيعُواْ ٱللَّهَ وَأَطِيعُواْ ٱلرَّسُولَ وَأُوْلِى ٱلْأَمْرِ مِنكُمْ$$

*O you who believe! Obey Allāh and obey the Messenger,*
*and those charged with authority among you.*
(*An-Nisa´* 4:59)

Rasulūllāh ﷺ is reported to have said:

*Hearing and obeying are the duties of a Muslim, both*
*regarding what he likes and what he dislikes, as long as*
*he is not commanded to perform an act of disobedience*
*to Allāh, in which case he must neither hear nor obey.*
(Transmitted by *Bukhāri*)

## WE HAVE LEARNED:

* Elders should be respected by those younger than them.
* Teachers have a special duty in this life and must be obeyed and loved.
* A good Muslim always obeys those who are in charge.

# EXERCISES

1. What did Rasulūllāh ﷺ say about honoring an elder?
2. Why should a Muslim respect his elders?
3. Why should a Muslim respect his teachers?
4. Why is it necessary to obey and cooperate with our leaders?
5. Can a group of people achieve anything good without coop eration and leadership?
6. What does the Qur'ān say about obedience to leaders?
7. What did Rasulūllāh ﷺ say about obedience to leaders if they order an act of disobedience to Allāh ﷻ?
8. How could you apply the teachings of this lesson in your daily life?

# LESSON 5

---

## KINDNESS TO ALL PEOPLE

### Kindness to Juniors

Ibn ´Abbas ⁕ reported that Rasulūllāh ⁕ said:

> *He is not one of us who dies without having shown kindness*
> *to our young ones and respect to our older ones.*
> (Transmitted by Tirmidhi)

Therefore, an older person should be kind to a younger one. He should not dominate him or be harsh with him. He should not hurt him or use bad words to mock him. Instead, one should be patient with the younger persons and set a good example for them. This way, he will learn to be patient with his juniors and also show respect to his elders.

At the same time, a younger child should be respectful of his elder brother or sister. He should try not to annoy him/her and make him/her angry. When his older brother or sister is working or doing something important, he should try to stay as quiet as possible and not cause distractions.

It is best to remember that mutual consideration and kindness is the basis of all Islāmic behavior.

### Being Good to All People

In Islam, every good deed is an act of charity and has a special reward from Allāh ⁕. Abu Hurairah ⁕ reported that Rasulūllāh ⁕ said:

*Enjoined on every part of human body is charity, every day in which the sun rises; doing justice between two people is charity; and helping a man onto his beast and leading it is charity; and a good word is charity; and every step which is taken towards prayer is charity; and removing harmful things from the road is charity.*
(Transmitted by Bukhāri and Muslim)

From this, we can see that a Muslim should try to be helpful and kind to all people, even if it is only by saying a kind word. Sometimes, this may be difficult, because some people are not always nice to you. At such times, you should remember that you will receive the reward for an act of kindness from Allāh, and that He is watching all your efforts.

Allāh especially likes the people who return evil with good. The Qur'ān teaches us that a good act always wins out in the end. The Qur'ān teaches us:

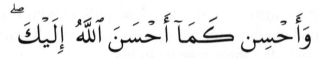

*Be kind, as Allāh has been kind to you.*
(*Al-Qasas* 28:77)

## WE HAVE LEARNED:

* We must show kindness and mercy to those who are younger than us.
* We must show consideration and respect to those who are older than us.
* Rasulūllāh taught us that all good deeds are acts of charity.

18

# EXERCISES

1. What did Rasulūllāh  say about kindness to young ones and respect for the elderly?
2. How should one treat his juniors?
3. Give five examples of how to show kindness and charity to other people at home and at school.

# LESSON 6

---

## TELLING THE TRUTH AND KEEPING PROMISES

### The Boy Who Cried Wolf

There once was a boy who was sent to guard his father's sheep outside his village. One day, he cried out, "Help! The wolf is killing the sheep!" The villagers rushed out to help him with sticks and guns. When they looked around, they found no wolf, only the boy laughing at them. The next week, he again cried, "Wolf!" and again, the villagers rushed out to him for nothing. Then, one day, a real wolf attacked his sheep. "Help!" he shouted. "The wolf is here!" But, nobody came to help him. He had told lies so often that even when he told the truth, no one believed him.

### The Girl Who Broke Her Promises

Maryam had a friend named Latifah. Latifah never kept her promises. Any time she promised to do something, she didn't do it. One time, Maryam told Latifah a great secret, and Latifah promised not to tell anyone. The next day, however, everyone knew Maryam's secret. Latifah had broken her promise, and Maryam never trusted her again.

Latifah didn't keep her friends for long, because she always broke her promises. Even when she would swear by Allāh ﷻ, nobody believed her. Soon, Latifah was very lonely.

# The Lesson of These Stories

It is very important to be truthful and to keep promises. Nobody believes a liar. Nobody trusts a person who breaks promises. Liars and untrustworthy people soon find they have no true friends.

A community without trust can never work together to improve their lives, because everyone questions the other's motives. Only people that are trustworthy can succeed in building a successful community.

# Rasulullah's Example

Rasulūllāh ﷺ was a very truthful and trustworthy person. Even before he was called by Allāh ﷻ to be His messenger, people liked his honest character. They even called him "Al-Amin", which means, "The Trustworthy", and As-Sadiq, which means the "Truthful One."

Rasulūllāh ﷺ is also reported to have said:

*If anyone is pleased to love Allāh and His Messenger, or*
*rather to have Allāh and His Messenger love him,*
*he should speak the truth when he says anything,*
*and fulfill his trust when he is in a position of trust.*
(Transmitted by Baihaqi)

# What the Qur'an Says About Truthfulness and Trustworthiness

The Qur'ān tells us to be truthful and trustworthy in many places. For example:

وَلَا تَلْبِسُوا۟ ٱلْحَقَّ بِٱلْبَٰطِلِ وَتَكْتُمُوا۟ ٱلْحَقَّ وَأَنتُمْ تَعْلَمُونَ ۩

*And cover not Truth with falsehood, nor conceal*
*the Truth when ye know (what it is ).*
*(Al-Baqarah 2:42)*

يَٰٓأَيُّهَا ٱلَّذِينَ ءَامَنُوٓا۟ أَوْفُوا۟ بِٱلْعُقُودِ

*O you who believe! Fulfill (all) obligations.*
*(Al-Ma'idah 5:1)*

يَٰٓأَيُّهَا ٱلَّذِينَ ءَامَنُوا۟ لِمَ تَقُولُونَ مَا لَا تَفْعَلُونَ ۝
كَبُرَ مَقْتًا عِندَ ٱللَّهِ أَن تَقُولُوا۟ مَا لَا تَفْعَلُونَ ۝

*O you who believe! Why say you that which you do not?*
*Grievously   hateful is it in the sight of Allāh*
*that you say that which you do not.*
*(As-Saff 61: 2-3)*

A Muslim must stop himself from telling lies. One lie often leads to others. Sooner or later, when the truth comes out, the only one hurt is the liar himself.  A Muslim must make sure that whenever he makes a promise, he keeps it to the best of his ability. Only then will others respect him and trust his word.

## WE HAVE LEARNED:

* A true Muslim is one who does not lie or break promises.
* People who lie all the time soon find themselves in trouble.
* Telling the truth gains the love of Allāh ﷻ and the respect of others.


## EXERCISES

1.  If someone tells lies often, will other people continue to believe him?
2.  Why is it important to keep promises?
3.  What is the meaning of the name ´Al-Amin´, and why was this title given to Rasulūllāh ﷺ when he was a young man?
4.  Explain the meaning of As-Sadiq?
5.  Quote the meaning of a verse of the Qur'ān or a *Hadīth* about truthfulness.
6.  Quote the meaning of a verse of the Qur'ān or a *Hadīth* about keeping promises.
7.  Give five examples of truthful behavior and trustworthiness.

# LESSON 7

---

## ISLĀMIC GREETINGS AND SALUTATIONS

### Greetings

Muslims greet each other with the greeting of peace. They say, 'As-salamu 'alaikum', which means: "Peace be upon you." The person replying should give the same greeting in reply: 'Wa 'alaikum as-salam', which means: "And on you, be peace," or a better reply: 'Wa 'alaikum as-salam wa rah-matulluhi wa barakatahu', which means: "And on you, be peace and the Mercy of Allāh ﷻ and His Blessings." Therefore, greetings between Muslims are very meaningful; they are prayers for peace and Allāh ﷻ's blessings and mercy on one another.

The Qur'ān advises us:

وَإِذَا حُيِّيتُم بِتَحِيَّةٍ فَحَيُّواْ بِأَحْسَنَ مِنْهَآ أَوْ رُدُّوهَآ

*When a courteous greeting is offered to you,*
*you meet it with a greeting still more courteous,*
*or (at least), of equal courtesy.*
(*An-Nisa'* 4:86)

Men may greet other men with a handshake. Similarly, women may shake hands with women. However, men and women should not shake hands with each other, unless they are closely related. They should only exchange vocal greetings.

# Visiting a Muslim's House

Rasulūllāh ﷺ advised us that when visiting a Muslim's house, the visitor should greet the people of the house from outside by saying, 'As-salamu 'alaikum'. If the visitor receives a reply and is invited in, he may enter.

If he calls 'As-salamu 'alaikum' and hears no answer, he may repeat his greeting in a louder voice. If there is still no reply, he may call a third time. After receiving no answer for the third time, he should leave. He should not go into the house or try to peep through the windows. He should respect the resident's right to privacy.

With all the resources of communication modern society provides, this advice of the Prophet ﷺ can be understood to mean that we should first phone our friend to see if it is convenient to visit. When we arrive at his house, we should ring the bell or knock at the door to inform him of our arrival and wait for the answer.

When a Muslim sees other Muslims or enters a room, he should also greet all those who are present with 'As-salamu 'alaikum'.

# When Visiting Non-Muslim Friends

Islam teaches us courtesy and friendly relations with all human beings. Our neighbors, both Muslim and non-Muslim have special rights over us. Each society has a form of greeting in which various members of the community greet each other. We must greet our non-Muslim friends with the greetings that are most courteous and most understandable. In Western societies, we may greet people with "Hi", "Hello", "Good Morning", "Good evening" etc. However, we should not use any greetings that are un-Islāmic and glorify anyone other than Allāh ﷻ.

# Greeting a Muslim When He Sneezes

If a Muslim sneezes, he should say, *'Al-hamdu li-(A)llah'*, which means: "All praises be to Allāh." Hearing the sneeze, others should say, *'Yarhamuka-(A)llah'* for a male or *'Yarhamuki- (A)llah'* for a female, which means: "May Allāh have mercy on you." And the person who sneezed should answer *'Ghafara (A) l-lahu la-na wa la-kum'*, which means: "May Allāh forgive us." So, even when we sneeze, Muslims pray for one another.

*Ya hadikumullah*

## WE HAVE LEARNED:

* Muslims should always greet each other with *'As-salamu ´alaikum'*.
* We should respect the privacy of others.
* When we sneeze, we should say *'Al-hamdu li- (A)llah'*.

## EXERCISES

1. How should one Muslim greet another?
2. How should a person reply to a greeting?
3. What is the meaning of these greetings?
4. Who may greet a man with a handshake?  Can women greet each other with a handshake?
5. How should a visitor approach a Muslim´s house?
6. What should someone say on entering a room where a Muslim is present?
7. (a) What should we say when we sneeze?
   (b) What should another person who is present say?
   (c) How should we reply?
   (d) What are the meanings of these expressions?

# LESSON 8

## ISLĀMIC MANNERS FOR MEALTIME

### Before Eating

Before eating, a Muslim should: (1) wash his hands; (2) say *'Bismi(A)llahi (A)r- Rahmani (A)r- Rahim(i)'*, which means: "In the name of Allāh, the Beneficent, the Merciful." This way he is reminded that it is through Allāh ﷻ's Mercy that he is blessed with food to eat.

### While Eating

While eating, a Muslim should:

1.   Use his right hand.
2.   Take food from the side of the dish nearest to him, and not pick at it, looking for the better pieces.
3.   Take a moderate amount of food on his plate, allowing others to have their fair share.
4.   Not waste food.
5.   Eat with other people if possible.
6.   Avoid gluttony and overeating.

Rasulūllāh ﷺ is reported to have said that when eating, one-third of the stomach is for food, one-third for drink, and the other third for air (i.e., it should be empty). If this advice is followed, a Muslim will derive many benefits from it for his health. The bad habit of burping will also be curbed.

It is inappropriate to burp in public. If one is overcome by gas, it must be done in private. If one is with other people, then he must turn his face to one side and cover it with his right hand. After burping, he should say '*Al-hamd u li- (A)llah*' (All Praises are for Allāh).

## After Eating

After finishing the meal, a Muslim must thank Allāh ﷻ and say:

*Al-hamdu li-(A)llahi (A)lladhi atamana*
*wa saqana wa (a)jalna min (a)l-Muslimin*

("All praises are due to Allāh who gave us to eat and to drink
and made us Muslims")

He should then:

1. Wash his hands.
2. Rinse his mouth.
3. Preferably, clean his teeth with a *Miswak* or toothbrush.

## WE HAVE LEARNED:

* Allāh ﷻ through His Mercy provides our food.
* We begin to eat with 'Bismillah'.
* A Muslim thanks Allāh ﷻ for the food he has eaten by saying '*Al –hamdu li-(A)llah*'

## EXERCISES

1. Name two things a Muslim should do before he eats.
2. Name three things a Muslim should remember to do while eating.

3. Name three things a Muslim should avoid when eating.
4. Name four things a Muslim do after eating?
5. Why should a Muslim mention Allāh's name at the beginning and end of a meal?

# LESSON 9

---

## PUNCTUALITY AND PROMPTNESS

### The Meaning of Punctuality

Punctuality means to do things at the right time. It is a very important quality to have. Sometimes, even doing a good deed may be of no use, unless it is done at the right time.

### *The Boy Who was Always Late*

*There was once a boy named Hilmi. He wasn't a bad boy, but his biggest shortcoming was that he was always late. At school, he would be late for class. If he had homework, it would never be ready on time. If his mother asked him to do something, he would reply, "Just a minute", and by the time he came, it was always too late to help.*

*He would get up late in the morning and offer his Fajr prayer late, even after sunrise! If he had to catch a bus or train, he would always miss it.*

*Many people blamed him, warned him, even beat him up, but nothing affected his tardiness.*

*One night, Hilmi had a dream. He dreamed about the Day of Judgment. To his joy, he found that he was among the people who had done good and would enter Paradise. However, when the time came to enter the gates of Paradise, Hilmi had somehow gotten delayed on the way. He suddenly noticed that the others of his group were already in the lovely garden, and he hastened to join them. But alas! Just as he drew near, the gates of*

*Paradise closed, and he was left outside. He heard a voice calling, "You're too late!"*

*Then, someone shook him to wake him up. It was his mother. "Hilmi, you are late for school again! Get up at once!" Hilmi realized then that it was not too late to change, and from that day forward, he was never late again.*

## The Need for Punctuality

A Muslim knows two things are inevitable: the Day of Judgment and death. He also knows that they can come at any time, without warning, so he should try to make the best of the moment at hand. This is why punctuality is so vital.

Also, when a person does not respect time, he makes life difficult for himself and for those with whom he associates, both at home and at work. His parents will be upset with him, because he does not do his chores on time. They cannot depend on him for any help.

His teachers will be angry, because he will delay the whole class with his tardiness. When he turns in a late assignment, he falls behind the rest of the class. When applying to college, if he is late in turning in applications for admission or scholarships, he may lose his chance to someone who is more prompt.

If he is late on the job, he may not get promotion or even be laid off, because he is not reliable. In business, if a person is late delivering orders or in making payments, he will lose all his customers to more reliable competitors.

Most importantly, if a person is always late for prayers, Allāh ﷻ will not be pleased with him, because he does not respect His Commands.

In every aspect of life, one can see that being punctual shows respect for yourself, for those you deal with, and above all, for Allāh ﷻ.

## Do a Good Deed at the Right Time

If you have any duty, it should be completed at its appropriate time. People will appreciate your action, and Allāh ﷻ will also reward you generously.

If you wish to do a good deed, do it promptly and don't delay. Allowing time to pass gives *Shaiṭān* the opportunity to distract you from completing it.

Allāh ﷻ says that if someone just intends to do a good action, he will get a reward. But, if he actually does the good action, he will get ten times that reward. Therefore, we hasten to do every good deed and not be late.

## WE HAVE LEARNED:

* There are many bad things that can happen to us if we are always late.
* Being late for Salah is a very disliked action in Islam.
* We must try to do good deeds as soon as the opportunity comes.

## EXERCISES

1. Name some of the results of not being punctual.
2. Tell the story of Hilmi in your own words.
3. Why should we be prompt in doing good deeds?
4. Delay in keeping appointments is a sign of disrespect for other people, and lateness for prayer is a sign of disrespect for the commands of _____ (Complete the sentence.)
5. Name some ways in which you can improve your punctuality for school or for any other activity.

# LESSON 10

## CHOOSING THE COMPANY ONE KEEPS

### Good and Bad Company

It is very important to choose your friends carefully, because the way they behave will have an influence on the way you behave. Good friends will encourage you to do good deeds and warn you against bad behavior. Allāh ﷻ advises us in the Qur'ān:

*O Believers, be careful of your duty to Allāh,*
*and be with the truthful people.*
(*At-Tawbah* 9:119)

The company of the truthful friends will encourage you to fulfill your duties to Allāh ﷻ and help you keep on the straight path of Islam. On the contrary, bad friends can persuade you to do things you know are wrong. Rasulūllāh ﷺ is reported to have said:

> *The best friend in the sight of Allāh*
> *is he who is the well-wisher of his companions.*
> (Transmitted by Tirmidhi)

One is known by the company he keeps. As Rasulūllāh ﷺ said:

> *A person generally follows the way of his close friends;*
> *Everyone must judge a person by the company he keeps.*
> (Transmitted by Abu Da'wud)

In other words, if you cannot make good friends, it is best not to make friends at all. Friends are important, but being the best person you can be is more important. Therefore, while having friends can be a good thing, you can also enjoy being by yourself sometimes.

## What Makes a Good Friend?

There is a famous saying that reads: "Birds of a feather flock together." This is used to mean that just as birds of the same kind fly together, human beings also choose friends with common interests and goals.

When choosing friends, one should first think, "Does this person have qualities that I admire?" Admirable qualities should include high standards of Islāmic *Tahdhīb*. If we keep the company of those who are well-behaved, we shall also be encouraged to behave properly. Such children are kind and helpful to others; they do their duties and have good habits for work and play. If they see someone doing something wrong, they try to stop them or warn them to stop. They do not join wrong-doers. A good friend is someone you can trust to always stand by you and not take advantage of you for his or her own benefit or popularity. By sharing the company of good people, we can improve ourselves using their example, and similarly, they may learn from our example.

However, if we join the company of those who are known to behave badly, we may slip into bad habits as well. For example, some children are unkind and disrespectful. Some quarrel and abuse people, or spread rumors about people behind their backs. Others may even be dishonest in their games. They are cruel to people and to animals. Their main purpose is to have fun, even if it is at the expense of others. Sometimes, we may be tempted to make friends with such people, because they seem to be popular. However, they are very unpopular with Allāh ﷻ, and His is the only pleasure we should seek.

## WE HAVE LEARNED:

* People who are alike usually choose each other as friends.
* We should never have friends who will have a bad influence on us.
* People are affected by the company they keep.

## EXERCISES

1. What did Rasulūllāh ﷺ say about good and bad companions?
2. What is the meaning of the proverb, "Birds of a feather flock together"?
3. What is the likely result of making friends with good people?
4. What is the likely result of making friends with bad people?
5. Why is it better to stay alone than to have bad friends?

# LESSON 11

---

## HELPING THE NEEDY

### Helping Those in Need is a Duty

Life is full of joys and sorrows. At one time or another, everyone experiences his share of happy times and sad moments. We know it is our duty to thank Allāh ﷻ for our happiness and pray for His help and forgiveness in times of sadness. However, it is also our Islāmic duty to help others who may be experiencing difficult times. It is the duty of the strong to help the weak. It is the duty of the rich to help the poor. It is the duty of the healthy people to visit and comfort the sick. It is the duty of everyone to take care of the less fortunate, particularly orphans and widows. By sharing good and bad times, we become more than a community, we become a brotherhood.

### Why People Need Help

Many unforeseen circumstances occur in life, which leave people in need of help. Allāh ﷻ tests the sincerity of our faith through such circumstances. For example, natural disasters, such as fires, earthquakes, hurricanes, and tornados, leave people homeless, without food or any belongings. Often, they have to rebuild their lives from almost nothing.

Due to unstable economy, people may lose their jobs, as companies close down. Sometimes, people become disabled due to illness or an accident and lose the capacity to work. Their families may suffer great losses as a result.

One can never tell when situations may change for the worse. Therefore, we should always be generous to those who are going through hard times and thank Allāh ﷻ for His Mercy.  Especially in times of prosperity, we must have compassion and sympathy for those who are suffering.

The Qur'ān says this about helping the needy:

وَمَا لَكُمْ لَا تُقَـٰتِلُونَ فِى سَبِيلِ ٱللَّهِ وَٱلْمُسْتَضْعَفِينَ مِنَ ٱلرِّجَالِ وَٱلنِّسَآءِ وَٱلْوِلْدَٰنِ ٱلَّذِينَ يَقُولُونَ رَبَّنَآ أَخْرِجْنَا مِنْ هَـٰذِهِ ٱلْقَرْيَةِ ٱلظَّالِمِ أَهْلُهَا وَٱجْعَل لَّنَا مِن لَّدُنكَ وَلِيًّا وَٱجْعَل لَّنَا مِن لَّدُنكَ نَصِيرًا ۝

*And why should ye not fight in the cause of Allāh and of those who, being weak, are ill-treated (and oppressed) who are asking:  Our Lord, rescue us from this town of oppressors and make for your presence protectors and provide us the defenders.*
(*An-Nisa´* 4: 75)

Rasulūllāh ﷺ confirmed:

*Allāh will not show mercy to him*
*who does not show mercy to others.*
(Transmitted by Bukhāri and Muslim)

The Qur'ān and *Ḥadīth*  especially mention the rewards of helping widows and orphans.  When a woman loses her husband, she is left without any support.  Her welfare and honor should be protected by all members of the community.  As Rasulūllāh ﷺ said:

*He who strives on behalf of a widow or a poor person*
*is like one who strives in Allāh´s path.*
(Transmitted by Bukhāri.)

When a child loses his parents, he is left with no one to care for him. Rasulullāh ﷺ, himself, was an orphan, and he made it a point to always love orphans. Making sure that orphans receive a proper Islāmic upbringing is an act of great reward.

Allāh ﷻ says in the Qur'ān:

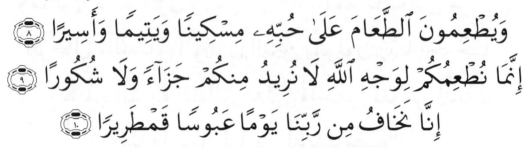

*And they feed, for the love of Allāh, the indigent, the orphan,*
*and the captive, (saying), We feed you for the sake of Allāh alone:*
*no reward do we desire from you nor thanks.*
*We only fear a Day of frowning and distress from the side of our Lord.*
(*Al-Insan* 76: 8:10)

Furthermore, Rasulūllāh ﷺ is reported to have said:

*I, and the one who takes responsibility for an orphan,*
*whether of his own kind or of others',*
*will be in Paradise thus: (and he pointed his forefinger*
*and middle finger with a slight space between them.)*
(Transmitted by Bukhāri)

## Muslims are One Brotherhood

To a certain extent, every Muslim is responsible for the welfare of each member of his community. Through this kind of care and love, Muslims demonstrate that they are brothers and sisters in Islam. Rasulūllāh ﷺ characterized this brotherhood best in the following *Ḥadīth*:

You will see the Believers, in their relationships to each other ...
based upon mercy, love and kindness--- as a single body;
if one part of it gets sick the entire is restless and in pain.
(Transmitted by Al-Bukhāri and Muslim)

This does not mean that Muslims should not be helpful and sympathetic to needy non-Muslims. Rasulūllāh ﷺ, himself, was most helpful to his needy neighbors. However, Muslims are one family. As members of the same family, the first duty of Muslims is to help each other.

## WE HAVE LEARNED:

* A good Muslim is one who helps others in their time of need.
* Widows, orphans and the poor must receive our special attention.
* Muslims, wherever they live, need our help when they are in trouble.

## EXERCISES

1. Which kind of people need our help and support?
2. What did Rasulūllāh ﷺ say about showing mercy to others?
3. What did Rasulūllāh ﷺ say about helping a widow or a poor person?
4. What did Rasulūllāh ﷺ say about one who takes care of an orphan?
5. In what ways can help be given to an orphan, a widow and a sick person?

# LESSON 12

## KINDNESS TO ANIMALS

There are many kinds of animals in the world: mammals, birds, fish, insects, reptiles, etc. Some are wild, some are tame, some are big, some are small, some are dangerous, while others are playful. Allāh ﷻ created the animals for a purpose just as he created human beings for a purpose. Therefore, we should respect all of His creation and be kind to animals.

Allāh ﷻ has allowed human beings to use some of these animals to help in their work, such as horses, mules, dogs, oxen. Other animals, such as cattle, sheep, goats and chickens may be used for food.

But this permission to use animals for sustenance does not mean one can be cruel to animals, or make them work beyond their strength. It is wrong to kill animals without a serious reason.

The Qur'ān teaches us to respect the rights of animals:

وَمَا مِن دَآبَّةٍ فِى ٱلْأَرْضِ وَلَا طَـٰٓئِرٍ يَطِيرُ بِجَنَاحَيْهِ إِلَّآ أُمَمٌ أَمْثَالُكُم

*There is not an animal (that lives) on the earth, nor a being that flies on its wings, but (forms part of) communities like you...*
*(Al-An'am* 6: 38)

Although human beings are the most intelligent creatures on earth, Allāh ﷻ has granted animals varying degrees of intelligence, as necessary for survival. Many animals even show certain behaviors that are similar to human behavior. For example, monkeys have been proven to have maternal instincts similar to those of humans and are capable of rudimentary verbal communication. Dolphins have also been shown to communicate through sounds. Dogs and cats show caring behaviors, such as loyalty to their masters.

As stated in the verse above, animals have shown the tendency to form communities just as humans do. Although not as complex as human communities, animals of the same species live together, breed, and care for their young. In certain animal communities, different members have different roles. For example, in bees, the queen bee is the leader and mother of the communities, and the worker bees make the honey.

Incredibly, animals are spiritual beings also. If you listen very carefully to the sounds of crickets before dawn, or the chirping of the birds, you can hear a certain rhythm that sounds like Tasbih. The Qur'ān states that animals have their own ways of worshiping Allāh ﷻ:

$$\text{أَلَمْ تَرَ أَنَّ ٱللَّهَ يُسَبِّحُ لَهُۥ مَن فِى ٱلسَّمَـٰوَٰتِ وَٱلْأَرْضِ وَٱلطَّيْرُ صَـٰٓفَّـٰتٍ ۖ كُلٌّ قَدْ عَلِمَ صَلَاتَهُۥ وَتَسْبِيحَهُۥ ۗ وَٱللَّهُ عَلِيمٌۢ بِمَا يَفْعَلُونَ}$$

*See you not that it is Allāh whose praises all beings in the heavens*
*and on earth do celebrate, and the birds (of the air) with wings outspread?*
*Each one knows its own (mode of) prayer and praise.*
*And Allāh knows well all that they do.*
(*An-Nur* 24: 41)

Animals may possess an intelligence and awareness of Allāh ﷻ that we do not understand, so we must respect that they have certain rights on this earth.

## Slaughtering an Animal

When a Muslim slaughters an animal for its meat, he must do so with the

41

name of Allāh ﷻ. Declaring, *"Bismillāh Allāhu Akbar"* (In the name of Allāh, Allāh is the Greatest), he should slaughter the animal quickly with a sharp knife. He should not slaughter the animal where other animals can see and feel afraid. A Muslim only takes life for a serious reason, in a merciful manner and with Allāh's ﷻ name.

## Killing Harmful Animals

It is allowed to kill harmful animals, such as snakes, scorpions and mosquitoes, when they pose potential danger. However, killing for sport is not permissible.

## Killing Animals Without a Good Reason

It is a sin to kill any animal without a good reason. Rasūlullāh ﷺ is reported to have said:

> *Whoever kills a sparrow (a small bird) for nothing, it will cry out*
> *loud to Allāh on the Day of Resurrection, saying: 'O my Lord!*
> *This person killed me for nothing; he did not kill me for any good reason.*
> (Transmitted by Nasa'i)

## Stealing Young Animals or Birds' Eggs

It is reported that when Rasūlullāh ﷺ was on a journey he left *Ṣaḥābah* for a while. He saw a bird with two chicks. The bird was hiding its chicks and spreading out its wings in distress. When Rasūlullāh ﷺ returned to the place he asked people, "Whoever has pained this bird by taking her chicks: Return them to her."

Rasūlullāh ﷺ was trying to emphasize that animals have feelings of love for their young ones, just as human beings have. Therefore, we should not steal young animals or birds' eggs, just as we should not steal young children from their parents.

## Treating Beasts of Burden with Consideration

Beasts of burden are those animals that work by carrying or transporting people or goods for their owners. Without them, many people would have no means of transportation. Because they work so hard, it is important to be kind to such animals. Rasūlullāh ﷺ is reported to have said:

*Fear Allāh in treating animals, and ride them*
*when they are fit to be ridden, and get off them when they are tired.*
(Transmitted by Abu Da'wūd)

Therefore, a Muslim may not overwork an animal or whip it when it is tired. One should be considerate in providing adequate amounts of food, water, and rest from work to working animals.

## Taking Care of Domesticated Animals

It is reported that Rasūlullāh ﷺ heard of a woman who locked her cat in a room and gave it no food until it died of starvation. He commented that the woman would go to Hell because of her cruelty to her cat.

Rasūlullāh ﷺ also spoke of the case of a man who saw a thirsty dog and drew water from a well for it to drink. Rasūlullāh ﷺ observed that for his kindness to the animal, Allāh ﷻ would forgive his sins.

Pets can be a real joy. They are fun to cuddle and play with. They are loyal and protective. However, we must take good care of them by feeding them, giving them baths, cleaning up after them and taking them for walks in fresh air. When we play with them, we shouldn't be rough or hurt them. Just as we count on them for their love and friendship, they count on us to take care of their needs.

# Lessons to be Learned

From the above *Aḥadīth* and Qur'ānic verses, we can learn three important lessons. First, it is important to treat animals with consideration, as members of our world community. They were created by Allāh ﷻ and worship Him in their own ways. Second, cruelty to animals is a serious sin. Therefore, it is our duty to try to stop others, especially children, from acts of cruelty to animals, explaining to them what the Rasūlullāh ﷺ has said about it.

## WE HAVE LEARNED:

* Animals are Allāh's creation too and have certain rights.
* A Muslim can eat the meat of an animal only if it is slaughtered with the words *"Bismillāh"*.
* We should treat all animals with kindness and mercy.

## EXERCISES

1. What does the Qur'ān say about animals?
2. A Muslim may kill an animal for ———————— , or because it is causiing to human beings. _____
   (Complete the sentence.)
3. How should a Muslim slaughter an animal to avoid causing the animal unnecessary pain and fear to other animals nearby?
4. What did Rasūlullāh ﷺ say about killing animals for no reason?
5. What did Rasūlullāh ﷺ say about stealing young animals from their parents?
6. What did Rasūlullāh ﷺ say about the treatment of beasts of burden?
7. What did Rasūlullāh ﷺ say would be the punishment of the woman who starved her cat to death?
8. State various ways in which you can show kindness to a cat, a bird, a horse, a donkey, or any other animal.

# LESSON 13

---

## MODESTY AND HUMILITY

Modesty is purity of intention in all actions. A modest or humble person does good deeds without trying to get noticed or show off. The opposite of modesty and humility is pride.

## Modesty and Islam

As you may recall, Rasūlullāh ﷺ said: "Actions are judged by their intentions." Since modesty means purity of intention, it is also an essential aspect of Islāmic *Tahdhīb*. It is reported that Rasūlullāh ﷺ said:

> *Every religion has its special characteristics:*
> *the characteristic of Islam is modesty.*
> (Transmitted by Abu Da'wūd)

Basic to a Muslim's faith is the belief that the Supreme Creator of all things is Allāh ﷻ, and human beings are only a small part of His creation. By accepting that Allāh ﷻ is Almighty, and we are His servants, every Muslim is bound to humility and modesty. Rasūlullāh ﷺ said:

> *Modesty is part of faith, and faith leads to Paradise.*
> (Transmitted by Ahmad and Tirmidhi)

## Showing-off vs. Being Modest

No one likes a show-off. Show-offs want recognition for everything they do. They think that they are better than others and try to make others feel inferior. More than anything, they want to be admired. But, even when people pay attention to them, in their hearts, they do not admire them. They may envy them for their wealth, good looks, intelligence, etc., but they do not like them.

People take pride in different things. Some people are proud of being the son or daughter of an important person. Some people may be proud of being rich. Others may be proud of being beautiful. Still, others may be proud of being learned or intelligent.

Good heritage, wealth, beauty, and intelligence may all be wonderful qualities, but one should not lose sight of the fact that everything he has is a gift of Allāh ﷻ. Bragging shows ingratitude to Allāh ﷻ. Indeed, as easily as He gives His bounties, He can just as easily take them away.

## Why Do People Dislike Show-offs?

If a person has admirable qualities, they shine through his behavior. Boasting about one's own qualities diminishes their value. Instead of winning admiration, people may resent such a person. It is the person who quietly does good works that accomplishes the most and earns respect.

Sometimes, people do good deeds, such as giving charity or offering extra fasts, and brag to others about what good Muslims they are. Such people are not seeking Allāh ﷻ's pleasure; they are seeking the acceptance and praise of others. Unfortunately, in doing so, they may win the admiration of others, but they are losing the reward for the Hereafter. According to Rasūlullāh ﷺ, on the Day of Judgment, among the seven types of people Allāh ﷻ will take under his protection, one will be:

*He is most charitable who gives so secretly that*
*his left hand does not know what his right hand has given.*
(Transmitted by Bukhāri)

46

# A Muslim's View of Himself

A true Muslim knows that everything he has is a gift from Allāh ﷻ: birth, beauty, wealth, intelligence, etc. A true Muslim is grateful to Allāh ﷻ for all he has been given. He has nothing to be proud of, but instead, he has much to be thankful for. Therefore, he tries to use what Allāh ﷻ has given him to lead a decent, Islāmic life. He knows that Allāh ﷻ sees everything he does, and so, he remains humble before Allāh ﷻ and modest before other people.

## WE HAVE LEARNED:

* Modesty is a major characteristic of Islām.
*There are many reasons that may make us want to show off to others.
*A Muslim knows that everything he or she has is a gift from Allāh ﷻ.

## EXERCISES

1. What is modesty?
2. What did Rasūlullāh ﷺ say about modesty?
3. What things are show-offs usually proud of?
4. Why do other people dislike show-offs?
5. Is a true Muslim proud of himself or grateful to Allāh ﷻ?
6. Describe how you would avoid being proud at school, and play.

# LESSON 14

---

## DECENCY OF DRESS AND GOOD MANNERS

### The Purpose of Dress

In the last lesson, we discussed modesty. Part of modest living is decency in behavior, speech, and even the way we dress. Our dress not only affects how we look outside but also represents what we are inside. Allāh ﷻ says in the Qur'ān:

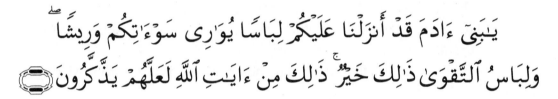

*O you children of Adam! We have bestowed garments upon you to cover your shame, as well as to make you look beautiful. But the garment of righteousness, that is the best. Such are among the signs of Allāh, that they may receive admonition!*
*(Al-Àraf 7:26)*

The main function of our dress is to cover our shame and enhance our outward appearance. Furthermore, being appropriately dressed brings out from within us a feeling of wholesomeness and modesty that may not be apparent to the eye but is obvious from our behavior. In Islām, our feelings of modesty and shame come naturally from Allāh ﷻ, and those who are true to such feelings are very dear to Him.

Dress has two more important functions for human beings. Just as animals have fur to keep the body warm, human beings need clothes to conserve body heat and protect them against changing weather. Unlike animals, however, human beings also need to cover their nakedness to preserve their dignity and provide comfort to their bodies.

The way a person dresses also affects his behavior. If one dresses modestly, he tends to behave modestly. Whereas, if one dresses indecently, he tends to behave indecently. This is why the Islāmic code of dress is so strict and such an important lesson in *Tahdhīb*.

## Islāmic Dress Code: *Ṣatr*

According to the Islāmicdress code known as *Ṣatr*, mature girls and women should cover the entire body, except the face and hands when they are out in public, or when men other than their close relatives are present. They may wear whatever they like in private. However, they should avoid nakedness, even in front of other women and close relatives.

Mature boys and men are required to cover the body between the navel and the knees at the very least. However, it is best to wear modest clothing. They should also avoid nakedness, even in front of other men and close relatives. Men are also forbidden from wearing gold jewelry and silk clothing.

Both men's and women's clothing should be loose and thick enough, so the shape of the body is not obvious.

## Modesty in Dress and Manners

Islām discourages nakedness and extravagance in dress and behavior. Even Rasūlullāh 	, the leader of mankind, lived very modestly. If he had desired, he could have lived like a king, having big feasts and wearing silken robes. Yet, he never had elaborate meals and dressed in very simple attire. He even shared in household chores. He never acted as if he was greater than anyone else, but his incredible qualities made him great in everyone's eyes. His modesty and humility endeared him to his people.

When one learns to live modestly, he no longer needs fancy clothing or jewelry, or extravagant cars and houses. Therefore, jealousy and envy never enter his mind, and the *Shaitān*'s temptations do not lure him as easily. He can stay focused on more important things, such as the remembrance of Allāh ﷻ.

## WE HAVE LEARNED:

* Islām has given us several reasons why we must dress modestly.
* Both men and women must dress according to the rules of Islām.
* Dress is a necessity of human nature.

## EXERCISES

1. What are the purposes of dress in Islām?
2. Which parts of the body is a Muslim woman to cover when she goes out in public?
3. Which parts of the body is a Muslim man to cover when he goes out in public?
4. Is it good for a Muslim boy to bathe naked with other boys?
5. Why is it not allowed for a Muslim to wear tight or transparent clothing?
6. Is it acceptable for a Muslim to be naked in front of close relatives?

# LESSON 15

---

## KNOWLEDGE

### The Purpose of Seeking Knowledge

Knowledge is the information that we use to perform daily functions and plan future actions. When a child is born, Allāh ﷻ gives him some basic knowledge known as instincts. For example, as soon as he is born, a baby automatically knows how to cry and move his arms and legs. As we grow older, our experiences teach us lessons in life. We gain more knowledge of the world and what our purpose on earth is. As we learn about the world and the natural laws that govern it, it becomes evident that there must be an all-knowing, all-seeing, all-powerful superior being who created life. We know this Being can only be Allāh ﷻ.

Because Allāh ﷻ granted us intelligence, it is our duty to seek knowledge, so we can understand what Islām is and how we can best worship and serve Him. Rasūlullāh ﷺ has said:

*The search for knowledge is a duty for every Muslim, male and female.*
(Transmitted by Bukhāri)

Therefore, it is the duty of every Muslim, boy or girl, man or woman, to seek knowledge. By studying Allāh ﷻ's creation, we feel a deep sense of awareness and respect for Allāh ﷻ as our Creator, and thus, strengthen our *'Imān*. The Qur'ān says:

إِنَّمَا يَخْشَى ٱللَّهَ مِنْ عِبَادِهِ ٱلْعُلَمَـٰٓؤُاْ إِنَّ ٱللَّهَ عَزِيزٌ غَفُورٌ ۝

" *....Those truly fear* Allāh , *among His servants, who have knowledge.....*"
(Al-Fātir 35: 28)

51

Knowledge also protects us from the pitfalls that the *Shaitān* may mislead us into. As Rasūlullāh 🕌 said:

*One scholar is harder on the devil than a thousand worshippers.*
(Transmitted by Tirmi<u>dh</u>i and Ibn Majah)

If we know how to recognize good from bad, we can avoid wrong beliefs and make an effort to win the pleasure of Allāh 🕌 through sincere worship and good deeds. One who struggles in pursuit of knowledge becomes very dear to Allāh 🕌. Rasūlullāh 🕌 confirms this:

*Whoever travels in search of knowledge is on Jihad until he returns.*
(Transmitted by Tirmi<u>dh</u>i and Darimi)

In addition to preparing for the Day of Judgment, knowledge is a valuable tool for living in this world. Allāh 🕌 has provided us many natural resources. Without knowing how to access these resources, life would be very difficult. We would not have many vital technologies, such as electricity, improvement of crops and farming techniques, building dams for irrigation and hydroelectric power, developing medicines to cure disease, among many others.

## The Value of Educators

Because they teach the fundamentals of knowledge, educators are greatly respected in Islām. Without good educators, students cannot develop a strong foundation for their knowledge base. In fact, Rasūlullāh 🕌 is reported to have said:

*The ink of the ʾalim (knowledgeable person) is more precious than the blood of the shahid (one who dies fighting for the cause of Allāh.)*
(Transmitted by Tirmi<u>dh</u>i)

Therefore, a knowledgeable person, or *ʾalim*, deserves respect and consideration, because as an educator, he provides an invaluable service to humanity.

## What is Meant by Knowledge?

A Muslim's knowledge base must include a thorough understanding of the fundamentals of Islām. In addition, one should be well versed in Islāmiclaw *(Shari'ah)*, the sciences, languages, mathematics, agriculture, medicine, arts and crafts, etc.

However, if in the course of his non-religious studies, the Muslim is taught something that is contrary to the teachings of the Qur'ān and *Hadīth*, he must follow only what Allāh ﷻ and His Messenger have said. We must never forget that Allāh ﷻ's knowledge is perfect and complete. The limited knowledge human beings do possess was also granted by Allāh ﷻ.

## WE HAVE LEARNED:

* The most important knowledge is that of our religion, Islām.
* Knowledge of all subjects is helpful to individuals and society.
* All Muslims must try to gain as much knowledge as they can in their lifetime.

## EXERCISES

1.  Why is knowledge so important?
2.  According to the Qur'ān, which type of people truly fear Allāh ﷻ?
3.  Explain some of the *Ahadīth* about knowledge and learned people.
4.  What sort of knowledge should a Muslim try to obtain?
5.  What steps can you take to become a well-educated Muslim?

# LESSON 16

## ISLĀMIC BROTHERHOOD

### The Meaning of Islāmic Brotherhood

A Muslim should treat other Muslims as his brothers and sisters, caring about their welfare, as he would care about his own family. The relationship is one of trust, love, respect, and companionship. Muslims should live together in peace, sharing their joys and their sorrows. Rasūlullāh ﷺ is reported to have said:

> *A Muslim is a Muslim's brother: he does not abuse him or*
> *abandon him. If anyone cares for his brother's needs,*
> *Allāh will care for his needs; if anyone removes his*
> *brother's anxiety, Allāh will remove his anxiety on the Day of*
> *Judgment; and if anyone hides a Muslim's weaknesses,*
> *Allāh will hide his secrets on the Day of Judgment.*
> (Transmitted by Bukhāri)

Upholding the Islāmicbrotherhood is a moral obligation for every Muslim and an important part of one's faith. Rasūlullāh ﷺ reported:

> *By Him in whose hand my soul rests, a man does not believe*
> *until he likes for his brother what he likes for himself.*
> (Transmitted by Bukhāri and Muslim)

### The Muslim Community Includes All Colors, Races and Tribes

Islām is truly the universal faith. One can find Muslims of all nationalities, living in every part of the world. They include Arabs, Iranians, Pakistanis, Malays, Chinese, Uzbeks, Turks, Africans, Bosnians, Americans and many hundreds of others.

The common bond of Islām makes Muslims of all races and tribes are brothers and sisters. They should love one another and help one another. They should not fight or quarrel with each other. Allāh ﷻ says in the Qur'ān:

إِنَّمَا ٱلْمُؤْمِنُونَ إِخْوَةٌ فَأَصْلِحُواْ بَيْنَ أَخَوَيْكُمْ

*The believers are but a single brotherhood: so make peace and reconciliation between your two (contending) brothers...*
(*Al-Hujurat* 49: 10)

The strength of the *Ummah* lies in unity. The *Shaitān* knows there is strength in numbers, so he tries to create divisions between Muslims to conquer our souls. We must avoid the tendency to group together on racial lines against each other, because that would be our downfall. Allāh ﷻ warns us in the Qur'ān:

وَٱعْتَصِمُواْ بِحَبْلِ ٱللَّهِ جَمِيعًا وَلَا تَفَرَّقُواْ

*And hold fast, all together, by the rope which Allāh (stretches out for you), and be not divided among yourselves.*
(*Aal-i-Imran* 3: 103)

We must remember that above all, despite differences in gender, nationality, or race, we are Muslims, and we share common faith in Allāh ﷻ and His teachings. There should be no stronger bond, and no other brotherhood can be more fulfilling.

# Islām Condemns Racism and Tribalism

Interestingly, every war in world history has been fought over nationalism and territorialism. The belief that one nation's people is superior to another is a man-made notion. Allāh ﷻ rejects any such divisions among his creation. Allāh ﷻ says in the Qur'ān:

يَـٰٓأَيُّهَا ٱلنَّاسُ إِنَّا خَلَقْنَـٰكُم مِّن ذَكَرٍ وَأُنثَىٰ وَجَعَلْنَـٰكُمْ شُعُوبًا وَقَبَآئِلَ لِتَعَارَفُوٓا۟ إِنَّ أَكْرَمَكُمْ عِندَ ٱللَّهِ أَتْقَىٰكُمْ

*O mankind! We created you from a single (pair) of a male and a female, and made you into nations and tribes, that ye may know each other (not that ye may despise each other). Verily, the most honored of you in the sight of Allāh is (he who is) the most righteous of you.....*
(Al-Hujurat 49: 13)

The only difference Allāh ﷻ sees between us is the purity of our faith and actions. Rasūlullāh ﷺ further emphasized:

*You are not better than people with red or black skins unless you excel them in piety.*
(Transmitted by Ahmad)

Therefore, there is no room for racial or national pride in Islām. Such pride is the creation of human beings, propagated by the *Shaitān,* and it only functions to break down the Islāmic brotherhood and distract us from serving Allāh ﷻ.

## WE HAVE LEARNED:

* All Muslims are members of one big family.
* Allāh ﷻ revealed Islām for every nation, race and color.
* A true Muslim stands against racism and prejudice.

## EXERCISES

1. How should a Muslim treat other Muslims?
2. Complete the following *Ḥadīth:* "By Him in whose hand my soul is, a man does not believe until he ————————— "
3. Name three races or nationalities of Muslims. Which is the best one?
4. Describe one of the ways some people look down upon others in a school, and explain the right way to correct that type of bad behavior.
5. Describe three ways you could show a fellow Muslim that you regard him or her as your brother or sister.

# LESSON 17

## GOOD RELATIONS WITH PEOPLE OF OTHER RELIGIONS

### We are All One Human Family

Islām is a religion of peace and good will. As Muslims, we believe that Allāh ﷻ is the Creator of everyone, and He sent His guidance to all the people of the world. Our Prophet Muhammad was sent as a messenger for all humanity, and he is Rahmat al- li al-Alamin," which means, "Mercy to all human kind." We believe that all humanity, no matter what color, origin or faith, is one family and must learn to coexist peacefully. Allāh ﷻ says in the Qur'ān:

$$إِنَّ هَـٰذِهِۦٓ أُمَّتُكُمْ أُمَّةً وَٰحِدَةً وَأَنَا۠ رَبُّكُمْ فَٱعْبُدُونِ ۝$$

*Indeed! this 'Ummah (Community) of yours is one
'Ummah and I am your Lord, so worship Me.*
(*Al-Anbiya'* 21:92)

### Islam is the Complete Way of Life for All

Allāh ﷻ sent many prophets and messengers before Rasūlullāh ﷺ. Unfortunately, misled people changed many of their teachings. Finally, Allāh ﷻ sent his last messenger with His final, perfect message, the Qur'ān. He promised to protect it from human distortion for the rest of eternity. The Qur'ān teaches us how to live as Muslims in submission to Allāh ﷻ. Muslims have a duty to invite others to Islām. We must learn how to present our way of life in a way that they can understand and appreciate it. The Qur'ān teaches us to practice what we preach and our own example can be the best teaching method in itself.

## Inviting People to Islam

Inviting people to Islām, or *Da'wah*, is a very important part of being a Muslim. Allāh ﷻ has provided us with some guidelines of the best ways of doing *Da'wah*:

ٱدْعُ إِلَىٰ سَبِيلِ رَبِّكَ بِٱلْحِكْمَةِ وَٱلْمَوْعِظَةِ ٱلْحَسَنَةِ
وَجَٰدِلْهُم بِٱلَّتِى هِىَ أَحْسَنُ

*Invite (all) to the way of thy Lord with wisdom and beautiful
preaching, and argue with them in ways that are best.*
(*An-Nahl* 16: 125)

Before we can invite anyone to Islām, we must be certain that we have our own facts straight. Because if we sound uncertain, we can discourage people from joining us and do more damage than good.

وَلَا تُجَٰدِلُوٓاْ أَهْلَ ٱلْكِتَٰبِ إِلَّا بِٱلَّتِى هِىَ أَحْسَنُ إِلَّا ٱلَّذِينَ
ظَلَمُواْ مِنْهُمْ وَقُولُوٓاْ ءَامَنَّا بِٱلَّذِىٓ أُنزِلَ إِلَيْنَا وَأُنزِلَ
إِلَيْكُمْ وَإِلَٰهُنَا وَإِلَٰهُكُمْ وَٰحِدٌ وَنَحْنُ لَهُۥ مُسْلِمُونَ ۝

*And argue not with the People of the Book, except in the best way,
unless it be with them who do wrong . And say to them we believe
in the revelation which has come down to us and that which has
come down to you, and your God and our God is One: and it is*

59

*to Him that we submit. to ...*
*(Al-'Ankabut 29:46)*

Allāh ﷻ teaches us to talk with other human beings kindly and seek common ground while talking to them. When talking to people of other faith we must start with what is common among us and not where we differ. We can discuss important matters of faith when we have established common ground and confidence.

It is also wrong to belittle the beliefs of others and ridicule their idols and gods:

$$ وَلَا تَسُبُّواْ ٱلَّذِينَ يَدْعُونَ مِن دُونِ ٱللَّهِ فَيَسُبُّواْ ٱللَّهَ عَدْوًا $$

$$ بِغَيْرِ عِلْمٍ $$

*Revile ye not those whom they call upon besides Allāh,*
*in case they out of spite revile Allāh in their ignorance...*
*(Al-Anam 6: 108)*

When we feel strongly about something so important as faith, it is easy to get excited during discussion with someone holding an opposing view. It is important to remember that you cannot force someone to see the truth if his mind is not open to the truth. The ability to see the truth with an open mind comes from Allāh ﷻ, and not everyone is lucky enough to be given this capacity. Using any form of compulsion is clearly prohibited. As the Qur'ān says:

$$ لَآ إِكْرَاهَ فِي ٱلدِّينِ قَد تَّبَيَّنَ ٱلرُّشْدُ مِنَ ٱلْغَيِّ $$

*Let there be no compulsion in religion: truth stands out clear from error...*
*(Al-Baqarah 2: 256)*

When speaking to people of other religions, we should point out that all the religions share certain ideologies. Islām shares the basic truth of *Tawḥīd* and its moral teachings with all the major religions of the world. Allāh ﷻ is the source of all truth. When people of any religion go back to their original teachings, they find that in fact, *Tawḥīd* is the basis of their earlier revelations. However, much of the truth of the earlier revelations is lost.

Islām is closest to Christianity and Judaism because these two religions, more than others, have preserved the truth of their revelations, and their books clearly prophesied the coming of Rasūlullāh ﷺ. When speaking to Christians and Jews, we should make it clear that we all believe in the same One God and that we acknowledge them as People of the Book, revealed to them by earlier prophets. The only difference is that we also believe Rasūlullāh ﷺ was sent to clarify and complete the truth of Allāh ﷻ's earlier revelations to humankind.

## Embodying Islām Through Practice

One of the best ways of keeping good relations with non-Muslims, while at the same time inviting them to Islām, is to treat them with respect. If people see that a Muslim is kind and helpful, fair and trustworthy, they will like him. Moreover, they will be interested to know more about the faith that guides him to be good.

Therefore, every Muslim should try to behave in an appropriate manner and show how Islām is the best religion in the sight of God. A good example often carries more emphasis than words. The Qur'ān teaches us fairness, justice, good speech, righteous actions and cooperation in all good deeds and forbids, ridicule, bad language, injury, injustice and backbiting. A believer must practice all the teachings if Islāmic *Tahdhīb* and *Akhlaq* when dealing with Muslims or non-Muslims. A Muslim must always remember that while he is responsible for bringing the message of Islām before those who have not yet been enlightened, guidance is ultimately in the hands of Allāh ﷻ.

## WE HAVE LEARNED:

* It is the duty of every Muslim to bring the message of Islām to others.
* Calling people to Allāh ﷻ and Rasūlullāh ﷺ brings blessings.
* The best way to show others the beauty of Islām is through our good behavior.

## EXERCISES

1. How should a Muslim invite a non-Muslim to Islām?
2. Name three things that a Muslim should avoid when inviting people to Islām.
3. Name two beliefs that Muslims share with Christians and Jews.
4. How can a Muslim embody Islām through his actions?
5. Describe three things that many Muslims do nowadays but which are prohibited in Islām, and suggest some steps that could be taken to stop or discourage them.

# LESSON 18

---

## ETIQUETTE FOR BUILDING AND MAINTAINING MASAJID

### What is a *Masjid*?

A *Masjid* is a place reserved for the worship of Allāh ﷻ. Allāh ﷻ does not want anyone else worshipped there:

$$وَأَنَّ ٱلْمَسَٰجِدَ لِلَّهِ فَلَا تَدْعُوا۟ مَعَ ٱللَّهِ أَحَدًا ۝$$

*And indeed the mosques are for (the worship of)*
*Allāh alone, so call not anyone besides Allāh.*
(Al-Jinn 72:18)

Building, visiting, and maintaining a *Masjid* is a work of great piety. The Qur'ān teaches us:

$$إِنَّمَا يَعْمُرُ مَسَٰجِدَ ٱللَّهِ مَنْ ءَامَنَ بِٱللَّهِ وَٱلْيَوْمِ ٱلْأَخِرِ$$
$$وَأَقَامَ ٱلصَّلَوٰةَ وَءَاتَى ٱلزَّكَوٰةَ وَلَمْ يَخْشَ إِلَّا ٱللَّهَ$$

*He indeed, he shall build and maintain the mosque of Allāh,*
*who believes in Allāh, and the Last Day, offers regular prayer,*
*and gives the Zakah and fears none except Allāh.*
(At-Tawbah 9:18)

*Masajid* (Mosques) are the Houses of Allāh ﷻ, and He teaches us the *Tahdhīb* of visiting and using them.

# Entering a Masjid

It is *Sunnah* to enter the *Masjid* with the right foot in first and say this *Du'a'*:

*O Allāh ! Open the doors of Your Rahmah (Mercy) for me!*

A person entering the prayer area should remove his shoes, so he does not bring in dirt from the street. The prayer rug of the *Masjid* must be kept especially clean as people offer their prayers there and make *Sajdah* (prostration) to Allāh ﷻ.

# *Tahiyyat al-Masjid: Sunnah* Prayer on Arrival at the *Masjid*

According to some scholars, every time a person performs *Wuḍū'* and finds a place to pray, it is *Sunnah* for him to perform two *Raka'āt Ṣalāh* silently. This prayer is called *Taḥiyyat al-Masjid*.

# Waiting for the Prayer

One should then sit quietly while waiting for the *Ṣalāt al-Jama'ah* (congregational prayer) to begin. There should be no games, unnecessary talking or noise. One should spend his time in reading the Qur'ān, remembering Allāh ﷻ and offering *Nawafil* (optional prayers).

When the *'Iqāmah* is called, he and the other worshippers should form straight rows behind the Imam. They should stand close to one another, leaving no gaps in between making straight rows.

The women should stand behind men making their straight rows or in their own special areas.

## After the Prayer

The worshipper may stay for additional *Nafl* prayer, or for meditation or recitation of the Qur'ān. He should avoid anything that is not an act of worship such as chatting, excessive greetings, doing business, eating, etc., while in the *Masjid*.

## Leaving the *Masjid*

It is *Sunnah* to leave the *Masjid* with the left foot out first and say this du'a:

*O Allāh! I ask you to bless me with Your Fadl! (Generosity)!*

According to the tradition of Prophet Muhammad , the reward of offering the Ṣalāh with *Jamàah* is twenty-seven times more than offering it individually. We must make special effort to go to the *Masjid* for all our prayers.

In the western world, the Muslim community is new and is establishing Islāmic Centers and *Masajid*. Islāmic Centers serve both as a *Masjid* and social center. These centers are established by the donations of the community and managed by its *Shura* (Consultation). We must generously donate our money, time and expertise for community work and cooperate in all those things that will help the new Islāmic community to grow. The things may not always turn out as we wish, but it is part of our discipline to follow the *Shura* and never give up working with other members of the community for the cause of Islām.

## WE HAVE LEARNED:

* The *Masjid* is the House of Allāh and is built and maintained by those who love Him and believe in Him.
* While in the *Masjid* we should not talk, play or make noise. We

should concentrate only on remembering Allāh ﷻ.

\* We must participate in all the activities of our *Masājid* and Islāmic centers.

## EXERCISES

1. What is the main purpose of a *Masjid*?
2. Why should a person remove his shoes outside the *Masjid*?
3. Upon taking his place in the *Masjid*, one may pray two *Sunnah Raka'at,* called _____ .
4. On hearing the *'Iqāmah*, what should the worshippers do?
5. What should a worshipper do after the prayer, and what should he avoid doing?

# LESSON 19

---

## USING THE BATHROOM

### Entering the Bathroom

It is *Sunnah* to enter the bathroom with the left foot and say:

(اَللَّهُمَّ إِنِّي أَعُوذُ بِكَ مِنَ الْخُبْثِ وَالْخَبَائِثِ.)

*Allāhumma innī a`udhū bi-ka mina (a)l-khubuthī wa (a)l-khaba´ith!*

*O Allāh, I seek refuge in You from the devil and all kinds of evils.*
(Transmitted by Bukhāri and Muslim)

### Leaving the Bathroom

When leaving the bathroom, it is *Sunnah* to leave with the right foot and say:

(اَلْحَمْدُ لِلَّه الَّذِي أَذْهَبَ عَنِّي الأَذَى وَعَافَاني.)

*Alhamdū li(A)llāhi (a)lladhī `adhaba ´anni (a)l-`adha wa ´afāni*

*Praise be to Allāh, Who has taken away from
me what is harmful and given me health.*

## Relieving Oneself in Private

We learned in earlier lessons the importance of decency and modesty.

When going to the bathroom, one should maintain privacy and avoid indecent exposure. Rasūlullāh ﷺ explicitly said:

> " . . . He who relieves himself should be concealed
> (from the view of others)."
> (Transmitted by Abu Da'wūd)

Urinating in the Standing Position

It was reported by Umar ﷺ that Rasūlullāh ﷺ once saw him urinating in the standing position and said:

> "O Umar, do not urinate while standing." So after that,
> Umar said, he did not urinate while standing.
> (Transmitted by Tirmidhi)

Therefore, one should avoid urinating in the standing position. It is indecent and likely to soil one's clothing or the toilet seat.

## Going to the Bathroom with Others

Islām prescribes a full code of proper dress. For both men and women there are private parts of the body that must not be exposed to others. When using bathrooms, toilets and swimming pools, beaches and other public places, we must be very careful in exposing our private parts to others. Rasūlullāh ﷺ said:

> Two people (or more) should not go out together to relieve
> themselves, uncovering their private parts and talking to
> each other. Allāh hates this.
> (Transmitted by Abu Da'wūd)

# Washing After Using the Bathroom

It is *Sunnah* to wash the private parts with water after going to the bathroom. One should use fresh water and wash the hands with soap, or rub the hands on the clean ground if no water is available. According to Islāmic tradition, clean earth is considered as pure as water.

# General Cleanliness of the Bathroom

It is essential that a Muslim observe cleanliness and modesty when using the bathroom. These hygienic practices keep our environment clean and prevent the spread of disease.

If one has no choice but to relieve himself outside, he should not choose a public place like a sidewalk, or a park, where other people are present.

Out of consideration for the next user, one should always leave the bathroom tidy. One should not drop anything into the toilet except toilet paper. After making the *Wuḍū'*, we may find water on the sink or on the floor. We should wipe it with a paper towel or cloth before leaving.

We must show special consideration when making *Istinja'* (cleaning private parts) or *Wuḍū'* in the public facilities. If there is an Islāmic meeting in a hotel or public meeting place, we often ignore the fact that there are other non-Muslims who are also using the same facility and would not appreciate our leaving the toilet and bathroom untidy and wet.

# Reading In the Bathroom

We must spend as little time as necessary in the bathroom. It is not to be used as a place for relaxation. Evil spirits and thoughts linger. Some people are in the habit of taking reading material and use toilet time in light reading. All useful knowledge is sacred in Islām. Sometimes magazines contain articles about Islām, Prophet ﷺ and Muslim countries mentioning Islāmic names and places. The habit of keeping literature in the toilet and reading it must be discouraged.

## WE HAVE LEARNED:

* Going to the bathroom is a natural part of life and it must be done in privacy.
* We should follow the Islāmic etiquette for using the bathroom.
* These rules help us to keep ourselves clean and be respectful to the rights of the others.


## EXERCISES

1. What should a person say when entering the bathroom?
2. What should a person say when leaving the bathroom?
3. Why is it wrong to relieve oneself in an open area?
4. Why is it wrong to urinate standing up?
5. Why is it wrong to go to hold a conversation or do reading while using the bathroom?
6. How does a Muslim clean himself after using the toilet?
7. Name three places that should be avoided to relieve oneself?
8. Why should the bathroom be left tidy after use?

# LESSON 20

---

## GRATITUDE, PATIENCE AND ENDURANCE

### Good and Bad Fortune

Everyone faces good and bad times during the course of his life. You may be able to think of some things that happened to you that made you happy, and others that made you sad. Facing hardships makes a person stronger. With every difficulty, one learns important lessons in patience and endurance.

### A Test from Allāh ﷻ

People have the tendency to forget Allāh ﷻ during the good times and return to Him during difficulties. A Muslim should regard both good times and bad times as a divine test. During good times, Allāh ﷻ tests us to see if we are grateful for His favors. During bad times, He tests our patience and faithfulness. Allāh ﷻ says in the Qur'ān:

وَلَنَبْلُوَنَّكُم بِشَىْءٍ مِّنَ ٱلْخَوْفِ وَٱلْجُوعِ وَنَقْصٍ مِّنَ ٱلْأَمْوَالِ وَٱلْأَنفُسِ وَٱلثَّمَرَاتِ ۗ وَبَشِّرِ ٱلصَّابِرِينَ ﴿١٥٥﴾ ٱلَّذِينَ إِذَآ أَصَابَتْهُم مُّصِيبَةٌ قَالُوٓا۟ إِنَّا لِلَّهِ وَإِنَّآ إِلَيْهِ رَاجِعُونَ ﴿١٥٦﴾ أُو۟لَٰٓئِكَ عَلَيْهِمْ صَلَوَاتٌ مِّن رَّبِّهِمْ وَرَحْمَةٌ ۖ وَأُو۟لَٰٓئِكَ هُمُ ٱلْمُهْتَدُونَ ﴿١٥٧﴾

71

*Be sure we shall test you with something of fear and hunger,*
*some loss in goods, lives, and the fruits (of your toil). But ive glad tidings*
*to those who patiently persevere - who say,*
*when afflicted with  calamity: To Allāh we belong, and to Him*
*is our return  - they  are those on whom (descend) blessings from*
*their Lord, and Mercy.  And they are the ones who receive guidance.*
*(Al-Baqarah 2:155-7)*

So, we should always be ready for Allāh ﷻ's tests, remembering that He will guide us through the good and bad times if we stay true to our faith in Him.


## Rasūlullāh's Word on Gratitude and Patience

Rasūlullāh ﷺ is reported to have said about a *Mu'min* (a true believer) that:

*Wondrous are the believer's affairs, for there is good in all*
*his affairs and this is so only for the Mu'min. When something*
*pleasing happens to him, he is grateful (to Allāh) and that is*
*good for  him, and when something displeasing happens to him,*
*he perseveres patiently, and that is good for him.*
(Transmitted by Muslim)

As Rasūlullāh ﷺ points out in this passage, gratitude and patience are the mark of a true *Mu'min*.  When something good happens, his first impulse is to thank Allāh ﷻ. When something unpleasant happens, he does not give up hope, nor does he impatiently question Allāh ﷻ. He knows that if he maintains his faith and sincerely prays to Allāh ﷻ for help and guidance, he will be rewarded, Insha' Allāh ﷻ. The Qur'ān advises us:

$$\text{يَـٰٓأَيُّهَا ٱلَّذِينَ ءَامَنُوا۟ ٱصْبِرُوا۟ وَصَابِرُوا۟ وَرَابِطُوا۟ وَٱتَّقُوا۟ ٱللَّهَ لَعَلَّكُمْ تُفْلِحُونَ}$$

72

*O believers be patient and be better than others in patience,
and support each other to do right, and be conscious of Allāh;
that you may succeed.*
*(Āli 'Imran 3:200)*

## WE HAVE LEARNED:

* All good and bad times come to us as a test from Allāh ﷻ.
* Allāh ﷻ sees how we react in these situations.
* A Mu'min is patient during bad times and thankful during good times.

## EXERCISES

1.  Everybody faces both good and bad fortune during his life time. (True or false).
2.  Give some examples of good and bad times you have faced personally.
3.  How should a Muslim regard good and bad fortune?
4.  If a Muslim experiences good fortune, he should be _____ to Allāh ﷻ.
5.  If a Muslim meets misfortune, he should not give up _____ .
6.  Give three examples of misfortune and describe what one should do in each case to show their trust in Allāh ﷻ.
7.  Give three examples of good fortune, and tell what one may do in each case to show his gratitude to Allāh ﷻ.

# LESSON 21

## FORGIVENESS AND RECONCILIATION

### Returning Good for Evil

If somebody does you harm, you probably feel upset or angry. In fact, your first impulse may be to hurt the person who hurt you. If he told lies about you, you may feel like telling lies about him. If he cursed you, you may feel like cursing him. If he was rude to you, you may feel like being rude to him.

In Islam, it is forbidden to retaliate a wrong deed by committing another wrong deed. Under any circumstances, lying, cursing and rudeness are wrong. By behaving as badly as the person who wronged you, you become just as bad as they are. However, Islam does permit you to seek redress through a court of law for any harm or hurt inflicted on you. It is the right of the person who has been wronged to seek justice; if he decides to be forgiving, he will receive his just reward, because Allāh ﷻ loves those who are forgiving.

It is important to learn to control one's anger and respond in a cool, well thought out manner. By exercising self-control and patience in such situations, one can often accomplish a more positive result, and even make a friend of the person who was initially a rival.

The Qur'ān says:

وَلَا تَسْتَوِى ٱلْحَسَنَةُ وَلَا ٱلسَّيِّئَةُ ٱدْفَعْ بِٱلَّتِى هِىَ أَحْسَنُ فَإِذَا ٱلَّذِى بَيْنَكَ وَبَيْنَهُ عَدَٰوَةٌ كَأَنَّهُ وَلِىٌّ حَمِيمٌ ۝

*The good deed and the evil deed are not alike. Repel the evil
deed with one that is better, then lo!, the, person who
was your enemy (may become) like a close friend.*
*(Fussilat* 41: 34)

A Muslim always tries to keep a broad mind and open heart when dealing
with offensive people. Sometimes, people may try to irritate you just to
make you lose your cool and see your reaction. This is the *Shaitān's* mischief. By remembering your manners, you can prove them wrong and
defeat the *Shaitān's* evil purposes.

## Forgiveness

Occasionally, we may unintentionally hurt someone's feelings. If we
know we are at fault, we should quickly repent and seek forgiveness from
Allāh ﷻ and the person we have offended.

Knowing that we all are capable of making mistakes, we should always try
to keep a generous and forgiving heart. If someone shows sincere repentance and asks for our forgiveness, we should forgive him. We should not
try to make him feel guilty and desert him as punishment for his mistake.
Rasūlullāh ﷺ is reported to have said:

> *It is not allowable for a man to keep apart from his
> brother more than three days, each of them turning
> away from the other when they meet. The better of the
> two is the one who is the first to give a greeting.*
> (Transmitted by Muslim)

All punishment and reward comes from Allāh ﷻ. Only Allāh ﷻ can judge
what is in people's hearts. Therefore, we must learn to give people the
benefit of the doubt.

# Reconciliation

It is natural for people who love each other to disagree once in a while. The best of friends can argue. Brothers and sisters may occasionally quarrel. Even parents sometimes disagree in certain matters. But, we should not let small differences of opinion break up relationships. Sometimes, it is more important to let things go and reconcile your differences than to stubbornly insist that you are right and lose a precious relationship.

We should also try to persuade other people to forgive one another and live in peace. There is great reward for those who strive for peace and preserve the Muslim brotherhood. Allāh ﷻ says in the Qur'ān:

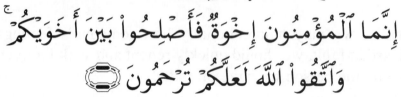

*The Believers are but a single Brotherhood: so make peace
and reconciliation between your two (contending) brothers;
and fear Allah that you may receive Mercy.*
(*Al-Hujurat* 49: 10)

# Making Peace

From the above teachings, we can see that making peace is a duty of a Muslim. A Muslim should be careful not to harm others. If someone hurts him, he should be the bigger person and treat him better than he has been treated. If the person who hurt him seeks his forgiveness, he should forgive him wholeheartedly. Finally, a Muslim should try to make peace between people who are in conflict with each other.

Peace and forgiveness are essential for the success of humanity. Allāh ﷻ loves those who are gentle and peaceful. Allāh ﷻ does not like those who cause trouble for other people. Rasūlullāh ﷺ is reported to have said:

*Have mercy on the dwellers of the earth -*
*the Lord of the Heaven will have mercy on you.*
(Transmitted by Tirmidhi)

## WE HAVE LEARNED:

* We have a right to seek redress for our hurt or harm but Allāh ﷻ loves those who return good for evil.
* A true Muslim strives for peace in all aspects of life and with all people.
* We should try to bring people together who have conflicts.

## EXERCISES

1. If someone harms you, how should you behave? Do you have a right to seek justice for any harm done to you?
2. If someone offends you, but is sincerely sorry, and asks you to forgive him, what should you do?
3. Is a Muslim allowed to stop speaking to or greeting another person?
4. If two Muslims are quarreling, what should you do?
5. Does Allāh ﷻ love those who cause trouble and refuse to live peacefully?
6. Describe three ways in which children offend one another at school or at home and describe how one could behave better in return.
7. Imagine that you came home unhappy from a hard day at school one day and started yelling at your little sister for no reason. She begins to cry. What should you do?
   (a) Make excuses and blame her for your crankiness.
   (b) Call her a baby for crying and tell her to be quiet.
   (c) Apologize for your outburst and try to make it up to her by doing something she likes.

# LESSON 22

---

## PREVENTING JEALOUSY

### What is Jealousy?

Jealousy is the hurt feeling we sometimes experience, because we long for something that another person has. We may feel as if we deserve what they have, and we are sometimes angry that we were not blessed with the same thing.

One may be jealous of others for all sorts of things: their beauty, their wealth, their popularity, for their clothes, their toys, or anything he wishes he had, too. A jealous person not only wants to possess what the other person has, but he wants that person to be deprived of his possession. Sometimes, he goes out of his way to hurt and harm the person who has received favors from Allāh ﷻ. For this reason, in *Surah al-Falaq* 113: 5 Allāh ﷻ teaches us to seek His refuge, *"...from the mischief of the jealous person as he practices jealousy."*

### Why is Jealousy Harmful?

Jealousy can be very destructive. It breaks up friendships and hurts people. In some cases, it has even started wars. But, how does jealousy begin?

Jealousy begins with resentment toward a person who has been blessed with Allāh ﷻ's bounties. A jealous person may steal or even try to harm the person to get what he wants. He feels that if he cannot be happy, no one else should be happy either. As a result, he may try to ruin another person's happiness.

78

However, what the jealous person fails to see is that when one is so consumed with anger and frustration, he leaves no room for happiness. He becomes blind to the blessings Allāh ﷻ has given him and concentrates on only those things of which he has not been given. Such ingratitude angers Allāh ﷻ, and He may withdraw His favors as punishment. Allāh ﷻ says:

$$ وَإِذْ تَأَذَّنَ رَبُّكُمْ لَئِن شَكَرْتُمْ لَأَزِيدَنَّكُمْ ۖ وَلَئِن كَفَرْتُمْ إِنَّ عَذَابِى لَشَدِيدٌ ۝ $$

*And when your Lord ordered: If you are grateful, I will*
*add more (favors) unto you; but if you show ingratitude,*
*truly My punishment is terrible indeed.*
(*Ibrahim* 14: 7)

It is important to remember that jealousy is a sneaky trap of the Shaitan. He uses jealous thoughts to create hatred between people. We must be careful not to fall prey to this trap.

How to Guard Against Feelings of Jealousy

Allāh ﷻ has a reason for everything He does. Sometimes, it seems that undeserving people have more in this world than the deserving, faithful people. Still, we must not feel jealous or angry:

$$ وَلَا تَتَمَنَّوْا۟ مَا فَضَّلَ ٱللَّهُ بِهِۦ بَعْضَكُمْ عَلَىٰ بَعْضٍ ۚ لِّلرِّجَالِ نَصِيبٌ مِّمَّا ٱكْتَسَبُوا۟ ۖ وَلِلنِّسَاءِ نَصِيبٌ مِّمَّا ٱكْتَسَبْنَ ۚ وَسْـَٔلُوا۟ ٱللَّهَ مِن فَضْلِهِۦ ۗ إِنَّ ٱللَّهَ كَانَ بِكُلِّ شَىْءٍ عَلِيمًا ۝ $$

*And in no way covet those things in which Allah has*
*bestowed His gifts more freely on some of you than on others......*
*(An-Nisa' 4: 32)*

This is Allāh ﷻ's test. As Muslims, our main purpose is to submit to the will of Allāh ﷻ. This means we must be thankful for His blessings and patiently accept the things we are deprived of. Allāh ﷻ promises great rewards for these sacrifices.

Still sometimes, it is difficult not to let feelings of jealousy take over. Instead of looking at people more fortunate than us and feeling deprived, Rasūlullāh ﷺ advised that we should look at those less fortunate than us and feel blessed:

*When one of you sees another who is better off than him*
*in respect of wealth and creation, let him look to one which*
*is below him, That is more proper that you do not hold in*
*contempt the favor of Allah towards you.*
(Transmitted by Bukhāri and Muslim)

As we discussed in Lesson 17, every Muslim is morally bound to preserve the Islamic brotherhood. According to Rasūlullāh ﷺ , if a Muslim sincerely considers every other Muslim his brother or sister, he should wish for him what he wishes for himself:

*By Him in whose hand my soul is, a man does not believe*
*until he likes for his brother what he likes for himself.*
(Transmitted by Bukhāri and Muslim)

When a Muslim finds happiness in his brother's happiness, feelings of jealousy never arise.

We should also realize that Allāh ﷻ has been kind and just to all His creations. If He has favored someone with something, He has also favored us also with many unique gifts. If we were deprived of any of these gifts of Allāh ﷻ, we would be at a loss. If we like something someone has, we should try to fulfill our desire with something equally satisfying. If we secure it, we should thank Allāh ﷻ. If we do not, we must remain patient, for Allāh ﷻ knows best what is good, and what is bad for us.

## WE HAVE LEARNED:

* Jealousy is the feeling of hurt by the happiness and favors of others.
* We should never feel jealous to others and always be happy and thankful with whatever Allāh ﷻ has given us.
* Allāh ﷻ and Rasūlullāh ﷺ have provided us with ways to guard against jealousy.

## EXERCISES

1.  What is jealousy? Give three examples of things people can make people jealous.
2.  How does jealousy lead to hatred and ungratefulness to Allāh ﷻ?
3.  In which Surah does Allāh ﷻ teach us to seek His refuge from the jealousy of the jealous person?
4.  Cite a Hadith that warns us to guard against jealousy.
5.  How might you prevent becoming jealous of others?
6.  Why should we accept the decision of Allāh ﷻ in all matters?
7.  Write a story of a jealous person who was hurt as a result of his own jealousy. Be sure to include how he repented to Allāh ﷻ and became a good Muslim.

# LESSON 23

---

## CONTROLLING ANGER

One day, a man met Rasūlullāh 🕌 and asked him to give him the most important rule of behavior. It is reported that Rasūlullāh 🕌 replied:

> *"Do not be angry," and he repeated this several times.*
> (Transmitted by <u>Bukh</u>āri)

Rasūlullāh 🕌 repeated his advice to emphasize how important it is to control anger. He was known to be very patient and calm, never letting anger rule his actions or words. This is one of the reasons why his followers felt so comfortable with him. Even the disbelievers respected him for his great patience.

## <u>The Harm of Anger</u>

Anger is probably the most destructive human emotion. Often, when a person gets angry, he can say and do things he may live to regret. He loses self-control. Out of frustration, he may shout, curse, and say awful things. He could hurt or even kill someone in extreme circumstances. When a person gets angry, he can do irreparable damage to himself and others.

Anger is another trap from the Shaitan to break our faith. Rasūlullāh 🕌 warned:

> *Anger comes from the <u>Shait</u>ān; the Shaitan was created from fire,*
> *and fire is extinguished only with water; so when one of you*
> *becomes angry, he should perform Wudu'.*
> (Transmitted by Abu Da´wud)

We must be careful to control our anger and not let our anger control us.

## How to Control Anger

Anger is a natural emotion. Certain situations can make anyone angry. However, one must know how to express anger in a constructive rather than destructive way. The best way is to stop and think about what you are about to do before you lose control. Then, try to convey your feelings calmly. You will find that you can make your point more effectively this way.

Rasūlullāh ﷺ gave the following advice in regards to controlling anger:

*When one of you is angry while standing, let him sit down; and if*
*his anger goes away (it is good); otherwise let him lie down.*
(Transmitted by Abu Da'wud)

When you learn to control your anger, you feel better about yourself, and others feel more comfortable around you.

## A Strong Person Controls his Anger

According to a Hadith transmitted by Muslim, Rasūlullāh ﷺ asked his Sahabah : "Who do you think is strong or powerful?"

They replied: "He who throws people down."

"No," said Rasūlullāh ﷺ, "It is he who controls himself when he is angry." Truly, it takes a great deal of inner-strength to control one's anger, because many times, it arises so suddenly that it takes us by surprise. This is why we should be aware of situations that can make us angry. Similarly, we should avoid doing anything to anger others.

# Allah Rewards Those Who Control Their Anger

Allāh ﷻ has promised that on the Day of Judgment, He will reward those who do not let their anger rule their actions. Rasūlullāh ﷺ said:

*Whoever controls his anger, while he has the power to show it,*
*Allah will call him on the Day of Resurrection*
*before all Creation, and reward him greatly.*
(Transmitted by Abu Da′wud and Tirmidhi)

The Qur'ān promises that those who control their anger are among those whom Allāh ﷻ loves:

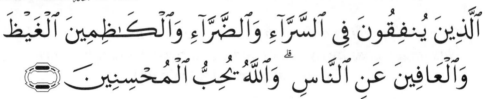

*Those who spend generously in ease and in difficulty,*
*and those who control their anger.*
*And are forgiving toward people:*
*Surely Allāh loves those who do good.*
(Āli 'Imran 3:134)

## WE HAVE LEARNED:

* Anger sometimes leads to many acts that one regrets later.
* Rasūlullāh ﷺ gave us his advice on how to control anger.
* Allāh ﷻ loves and rewards those who control their anger.

# EXERCISES

1. What did Rasūlullāh ﷺ reply to the man who asked him for a rule of behavior?

2. How might a person behave when he is angry?

3. What did Rasūlullāh ﷺ advise that an angry person should do to control his anger?

4. Which type of person did Rasūlullāh ﷺ say was strong and powerful?

5. Describe three things that annoy you the most, and explain what you would do in each case to control your anger.

6. Allāh ﷻ loves those who have the following characteristics:
   i.
   ii.
   iii.

7. Write a story about an angry person who got into trouble because of his temper.

# LESSON 24

---

## JUSTICE AND FAIRNESS

### The Meaning of Justice and Fairness

Justice and fairness means that all people should be given equal treatment. A Muslim has a moral responsibility to be just and fair in all his actions to all people---Muslims and non-Muslims alike. In everything he does, one should make certain that his decision is equally beneficial for everyone involved. Even if one tries to fool himself into believing that something unjust is just, Allāh ﷻ notes his every action and will question him on the Day of Judgment for it.

### A Justly Balanced *'Ummah*

The Muslim *'Ummah*, as a community, has a special responsibility to be just and fair. The Qur'ān reminds us:

$$\text{وَكَذَٰلِكَ جَعَلْنَٰكُمْ أُمَّةً وَسَطًا لِّتَكُونُوا۟ شُهَدَآءَ عَلَى ٱلنَّاسِ وَيَكُونَ ٱلرَّسُولُ عَلَيْكُمْ شَهِيدًا}$$

*And thus we have made out of you a justly balanced 'Ummah (Community), that you be a witness over the nations, and the Messenger be a witness over you."*
(*Al-Baqarah* 2:143)

For a person to be a witness over the actions of others requires that he be a just, upright citizen himself. In Rasūlullāh ﷺ, we had the best example of a just person. Even his worst enemies recognized that he was an honest, just, truthful and trustworthy person, because he maintained the same high standard of integrity with everyone equally. Many Jews of Madinah brought their affairs to him, knowing that he would always be fair.

A Muslim should follow the example of Rasūlullāh ﷺ and be an example to others in all matters of life, especially in matters of fairness and justice.

# An Example of Injustice

We all have had experiences when we feel we have not been treated justly, and others have violated our rights. We seldom realize that others may feel the same toward us. Let us consider the following example:

> *The class monitor, Rasheed, hears his classmates, Meksud and Arif, making noise. He should write down both their names in his report. Instead, Rasheed writes down only Meksud's name, because Arif is his friend. As a result, Meksud receives punishment, and Arif gets off free.*

The monitor is guilty of favoritism, and this is dishonest. The teacher left him in charge, trusting that he would be fair. He has not only done an injustice to Meksud, he has also done an injustice to the teacher and the rest of the class. Let's look at what happened next:

> *The next time the teacher left the room with Rasheed in charge, Arif started making noise again. This time, he is even more unruly. He knows that his friend won't report him, so he continues to disturb the class and doesn't worry about getting in trouble. Meksud stays quiet, because he learned his lesson the last time. Then unexpectedly, the teacher came back to get something and caught Arif in his mischief. She asks Rasheed to give her his report, but she notices Arif's name is not on it.*

*She questions Rasheed. Realizing that he has unjustly favored his friend, she decides that Rasheed is not reliable enough to hold the position of class monitor. Instead, she gives the job to Meksud, who, by learning his lesson, showed that he was responsible.*

# The Importance of Justice and Fairness

Anybody who holds a position of responsibility should be just and fair. Whether he is a class monitor, a chief, a principal, a governor, a supervisor, a manager, a judge, an Imam or president. People have the right to expect any person holding a position of responsibility to be fair and impartial. They count on him for justice. A leader should not favor anyone for their wealth, prestige, or heritage, nor should he be biased against someone for their racial background, social status, or for any other reason.

If a leader is unjust, people will not trust him. They will not respect him, and may even refuse to cooperate with him. He will set a bad example for the community. As a result, the whole society will suffer. On the other hand, a just and fair leader will be trusted by all. He will earn their respect and cooperation.

Similarly, a person who is called as a witness should tell the whole truth, and avoid bias or prejudice of any kind. In this way, he will be helping the cause of justice, fairness and happiness of many people.

We all must be just and fair in our daily dealings with people. For example, if someone owns a store, and gives the best goods only to his friends, he is being unfair. Similarly, if you share your cookies with your brother and not your sister, you are being unfair. Even if you treat one friend with more kindness than another friend, you are being unfair. We should always try to treat people the way we would like to be treated ourselves.

# The Qur'an on Justice

Allāh ﷻ says in the Qur'ān:

يَـٰٓأَيُّهَا ٱلَّذِينَ ءَامَنُوا۟ كُونُوا۟ قَوَّٰمِينَ بِٱلْقِسْطِ شُهَدَآءَ لِلَّهِ وَلَوْ عَلَىٰٓ أَنفُسِكُمْ أَوِ ٱلْوَٰلِدَيْنِ وَٱلْأَقْرَبِينَ ۚ إِن يَكُنْ غَنِيًّا أَوْ فَقِيرًا فَٱللَّهُ أَوْلَىٰ بِهِمَا ۖ فَلَا تَتَّبِعُوا۟ ٱلْهَوَىٰٓ أَن تَعْدِلُوا۟ ۚ وَإِن تَلْوُۥٓا۟ أَوْ تُعْرِضُوا۟ فَإِنَّ ٱللَّهَ كَانَ بِمَا تَعْمَلُونَ خَبِيرًا ۝

*O you who believe! Stand out firmly for justice, as witnesses to*
*Allah even as against yourselves, or your parents, or your kin,*
*and whether it be (against) rich or poor, for Allah can best protect*
*both. Follow not the lusts (of your hearts), lest you swerve,*
*and if you distort (justice) or decline to do justice,*
*verily, Allah is well-acquainted with all that you do.*
*(An-Nisa´ 4: 135)*

In this passage, we are being advised that we should be ready to stand for
the cause of justice, even if it means we have to be a witness against ourselves, or against our parents and relatives. Many times, we tend to look
the other way, when it is our own relatives who are behaving unfairly.
However, we fail to consider that they might be willing to correct themselves if they had the benefit of good advice. It is our responsibility to help
them understand the difference between right and wrong. If we start
accepting wrongdoing just because we don't have the courage to correct
our loved ones, then evil practices and unjust habits become the acceptable norm of the society.

Everyone must face the consequences of their actions, no matter how
important or well known. When we exempt people with wealth, influence

and power from their responsibilities, we are giving rise to injustice and oppression.

The greatest reason for injustice is self-interest. Greed sometimes makes us do things that are unfair to others. Let's consider the following story as an example.

## *Jamil's New Shoes*

*One day, Jamil's mother gave him some money to go to the store. She specifically asked him to buy school shoes for himself and his little brother, Harrith. When Jamil got to the store, he found these really great shoes for himself, but they cost more than his mother told him to spend. He thought to himself, "If I buy cheaper shoes for Harrith, I can buy these for myself with the difference." Harrith, being younger, trusted his brother and didn't question his judgment. On his way home, Jamil was very pleased with himself and his new shoes.*

*The next day, the two boys were walking to school, both in their new shoes. Halfway there, Harrith tripped and fell, twisting his ankle. Alarmed, Jamil asked, "What happened?"*

*"My shoe broke, and I fell down," answered Harrith, crying painfully. Riddled with guilt, Jamil carried his brother home to his mother.*

*When he got home, he told his mother what happened, confessing that he had bought good shoes for himself and lesser quality shoes for Harrith. Disappointed, his mother told him, "Jamil, I trusted you to be fair, and Harrith did too. But because you were greedy, Harrith is paying for your selfishness now. You were unfair to him and owe him an apology.*

*You know, if you hadn't admitted your guilt to me, I would never have known. However, Allah ﷻ was watching you and knew your every intention and action. Therefore, you must pray for forgiveness from Him."*

*Jamil apologized to Harrith and his mother and prayed two Raka'at Nafl for repentance from Allah. From then on, Jamil learned that greed and selfishness can lead to terrible injustice.*

## WE HAVE LEARNED:

* A Muslim must treat everybody, whether Muslim or non-Muslim, with fairness and justice.
* People in positions of responsibility have a special duty to be just.
* Both individually and as members of the *'Ummah,* Muslims have a special responsibility to stand for fairness and justice.

## EXERCISES

1. Give three examples to show what injustice means.
2. If someone is called as a witness in a dispute between a rich man and a poor man, what should he do?
3. Give three examples of how a leader can inspire a sense of justice and fairness in his people through his own behavior.
4. What are two common causes of injustice among students, and what would you do as a student leader to stop such injustices?

# LESSON 25

---

## BACKBITING AND CURSING

### What is Backbiting?

Backbiting means to say bad things about a person when he or she is not present. It is a very bad habit, which Allāh ﷻ has strongly condemned in the Qur'ān. Allāh ﷻ says:

$$\text{يَـٰٓأَيُّهَا ٱلَّذِينَ ءَامَنُوا۟ ٱجْتَنِبُوا۟ كَثِيرًا مِّنَ ٱلظَّنِّ إِنَّ بَعْضَ ٱلظَّنِّ إِثْمٌ ۖ وَلَا تَجَسَّسُوا۟ وَلَا يَغْتَب بَّعْضُكُم بَعْضًا ۚ أَيُحِبُّ أَحَدُكُمْ أَن يَأْكُلَ لَحْمَ أَخِيهِ مَيْتًا فَكَرِهْتُمُوهُ ۚ وَٱتَّقُوا۟ ٱللَّهَ ۚ إِنَّ ٱللَّهَ تَوَّابٌ رَّحِيمٌ}$$

*O you who believe! Avoid suspicion as much (as possible), for suspicion in some cases is a sin: and spy not on each other, nor speak ill of each other behind their backs. Would any of you like to eat the flesh of his dead brother? Nay, you would abhor it. But fear Allāh, for Allāh is Oft-Returning, Most-Merciful.*
(Al-Hujurat 49: 12)

In this verse, Allāh ﷻ stresses His disgust with backbiting by comparing it to eating the flesh of one's dead brother.

### How to Avoid Backbiting

We should not backbite, and if we hear others backbiting, we should not join them. We should either correct them, turn the conversation to another topic, or just leave. If that is not possible, we should at least be silent.

Allāh has forbidden backbiting, because it can be very hurtful and ruin a person's reputation. When talking about other people, we should try to think: would I be able to say these things about this person to his face. If not, we should not be discussing such matters in their absence, because they don't have the chance to clarify or defend their actions.

## What is Cursing?

Cursing is a form of verbal abuse using vulgar words or to wish misfortune on a person. A curse can sometimes be conveyed by gestures of the hands. Cursing is disrespectful and indecent. Rasūlullāh repeatedly warned against cursing:

*Do not use bad language, for Allāh*
*does not like bad language or the use of it.*
(Transmitted by Bukhari and Abu Da'wud)

*The believer does not taunt, curse, abuse anyone, or talk indecently.*
(Transmitted by Tirmidhi)

The sin of verbally abusing people is so great that all the rewards one has earned from prayers, *fasting, Zakah, Hajj* and other religious duties will not erase it. Such a person is deprived of Allāh 's Mercy:

*A person who is rude and has a harsh tongue*
*will not be admitted to Jannah (paradise).*
(Sharh as-Sunnah)

Rasūlullāh also warned that those who wish evil on others:

*Whoever curses a thing when it does not deserve it,*
*causes the curse to return upon himself.*
(Transmitted by Tirmidhi and Abu Da'wud)

Therefore, we should learn to control our anger and our tongues, so that we do not harm others or harm ourselves.

## WE HAVE LEARNED:

* Backbiting is a serious sin in Islam.
* Using bad language is not a sign of a true Muslim.
* We should never curse Allāh ﷻ's creation.

## EXERCISES

1.  What is backbiting? Give an example. _____
2.  The Qur'ān says that backbiting is like
    (Complete the sentence.)
3.  What should you do if you are among other people who are backbiting?
4.  What did Rasūlullāh ﷺ say about bad language and cursing?
5.  According to a *Ḥadīth* quoted in the lesson, there is a fault that cannot be wiped out by the rewards of a person's worship. What is that fault?
6.  What happens to a person if he curses something that does not deserve it?
7.  Describe three occasions on which students easily abuse or curse each other and describe what you would do in each case to control your anger.

# LESSON 26

## SUSPICION AND SPYING

### What are Suspicion and Spying?

Suspicion is the feeling that someone is guilty of doing something wrong, although there is no clear evidence or proof. Spying means to keep watch on a person secretly to see what he does.

Suspicion and spying comes from mistrust. Often, if you expect the worst of someone, you will only see bad in his actions. On the contrary, if you expect the best of someone, you will see only the good in his actions. This is why Allāh ﷻ says in the Qur'ān:

يَـٰٓأَيُّهَا ٱلَّذِينَ ءَامَنُوا۟ ٱجْتَنِبُوا۟ كَثِيرًا مِّنَ ٱلظَّنِّ إِنَّ بَعْضَ ٱلظَّنِّ إِثْمٌ ۖ وَلَا تَجَسَّسُوا۟ وَلَا يَغْتَب بَّعْضُكُم بَعْضًا

*O you who believe! Avoid suspicion as much (as possible):*
*for suspicion in some cases is a sin; and do not spy on each other,*
*nor speak ill of each other behind their backs.*
*(Al-Hujurat 49:12)*

### What is Wrong with Suspicion and Spying?

Clearly, being unnecessarily suspicious of our fellow humans is bad and of a fellow Muslim is worse. We should assume that every Muslim is a true believer, and he knows the difference between right and wrong. We must give him the benefit of doubt. We should trust our brothers and sisters and not think the worst of them. We are not responsible for the thoughts and private actions of others. Everyone has a right to privacy. We should not spy on anyone to see what he or she is doing privately.

Everybody has his faults, and at one time or another, we have all committed mistakes and sins to some degree. People who are suspicious and spy into other people's affairs are considered sneaky or nosey, because they are always getting involved in things that are not their business. Our business is to correct our own faults, not to look for faults in other people.

## Are Suspicion and Spying Ever Necessary?

In times of war or social unrest, Muslims may be compelled to find out the plans of the enemy or of mischief-makers to take necessary precautions. It may also be necessary for law officers to investigate evidence if a person is committing or planning a crime. These cases are different than simply being suspicious or spying for no reason other than curiosity or mischief.

World politics is very complicated, and many times, foreign governments want people to spy for them. Professional spying is a highly paid business with many risks. But the greatest risk in spying for foreign agents is the loss of moral integrity and self-respect. Sooner or later, the government or society finds out, and the foreign spy is then sentenced and disgraced. A Muslim must maintain his dignity and avoid doing anything for a profit that is immoral and illegal.

## WE HAVE LEARNED:

* Suspicion and spying are two bad habits to avoid.
* There are some times when spying is allowed.
* We should worry about our own bad deeds over those of others.

# EXERCISES

1. What is meant by suspicion?
2. What is meant by spying?
3. What is a "busybody" or "nosey" person?
4. Why is it wrong to look for other people's faults?
5. What is a foreign agent, and who hires him?
6. What is wrong with working as a spy for a foreign country?
7. Do research and find out about true stories of foreign agents and write the story of one of them, or use your imagination to make up your own story of a foreign spy.

# LESSON 27

## PRIDE AND MOCKERY

### What is Pride?

Pride can have one of two meanings. It can refer to the feeling of pleasure and satisfaction over a job well done. Such pride is not necessarily a bad thing. It encourages us to do better.

Pride can also mean to regard oneself better than others while considering others inferior. We will discuss this kind of pride in this lesson.

A proud person sees himself as better than other people. He may think himself to be more powerful, handsome or smart. He may think himself more important, because he is wealthier, more intelligent, or more religious than others. Instead of recognizing that all of these qualities are gifts from Allāh ﷻ and being thankful to Him, he wastes his time in self-admiration and begins to believe that he can do no wrong.

Islam teaches us to be humble and modest. We must thank Allāh ﷻ for making all our accomplishments possible. Allāh ﷻ condemns pride and arrogance.

In the Qur'ān, Allāh ﷻ says about pride:

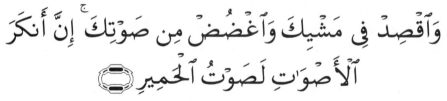

وَٱقۡصِدۡ فِى مَشۡيِكَ وَٱغۡضُضۡ مِن صَوۡتِكَ إِنَّ أَنكَرَ ٱلۡأَصۡوَٰتِ لَصَوۡتُ ٱلۡحَمِيرِ ۝

*And be moderate in your pace,*

*and lower your voice; for the hardest of sounds,*
*without doubt, is the braying of the donkey.*
*(Al-Luqman 31: 19)*

Here, Allāh ﷻ warns us about all kinds of showing-off in our manners, behavior and way of speaking. Talking loudly or boastfully is likened to the sounds a donkey makes. The analogy draws from the fact that donkeys are considered creatures of little intelligence.

## What is Mockery?

Mockery means to make fun of people in order to embarrass them or make them uncomfortable and unhappy. It means to laugh at other people because they are different from us or they don't belong to our group.

Mockery shows a total disregard for the feelings of others. Allāh ﷻ has specifically forbidden it in the Qur'ān:

يَـٰٓأَيُّهَا ٱلَّذِينَ ءَامَنُوا۟ لَا يَسْخَرْ قَوْمٌ مِّن قَوْمٍ عَسَىٰٓ أَن يَكُونُوا۟

خَيْرًا مِّنْهُمْ وَلَا نِسَآءٌ مِّن نِّسَآءٍ عَسَىٰٓ أَن يَكُنَّ خَيْرًا مِّنْهُنَّ

وَلَا تَلْمِزُوٓا۟ أَنفُسَكُمْ وَلَا تَنَابَزُوا۟ بِٱلْأَلْقَـٰبِ بِئْسَ ٱلِٱسْمُ

ٱلْفُسُوقُ بَعْدَ ٱلْإِيمَـٰنِ

*"O you who believe! Let not some men among you laugh at*
*others: it may be that the (latter) are better than the*
*(former). Nor let some women laugh at others: it*
*may be that the (latter) are better than the (former).*
*Nor defame nor be sarcastic to each other, nor call each*

*other by (offensive) nicknames: Ill-seeming is a name*
*connoting wickedness..."*
(*Al-Hujurat* 49: 11)

Therefore, we should never laugh at others for their shortcomings, because we are not perfect ourselves. In fact, they may be better than we are in the sight of Allāh ﷻ, so we have no right to judge. We should try to treat others with the same respect as we would like for ourselves.

People mock each other for various reasons. Sometimes, people use mockery as a response to their own fear of something or someone different; because they can't understand it, they make fun of it. Allāh ﷻ has created people of various colors, shapes, and sizes. They speak different languages. People come from many ethnic backgrounds. They may follow different religions. Yet, they are all part of His creation and very dear to Him. We must not do anything to hurt feelings of others or harm them in any way.

Sometimes, people are made fun of because they are physically challenged. Being blind, deaf, paralyzed, or mentally handicapped does not make them any less human than us. In fact, these people are special. They live with challenges on a daily basis with more courage and determination than most of us have. We should encourage such people with our love and concern and not support those who make fun of them.

In any society, people have different opinions on sociopolitical issues. Every opinion has its merits and flaws, so no one is necessarily completely right or wrong. Everyone has a right to an opinion, and we should respect the opinions of others. We may show our disagreement in a reasonable manner without ridiculing or laughing at them. If we give respect to others, they will respect us in return.

There is a famous saying: "Pride comes before the fall." One should never assume he is better than others, because sudden misfortune can hit at any time. The distribution of fortune and misfortune is in the hands of Allāh ﷻ, and we must not forget it.

## WE HAVE LEARNED:

* Being proud or arrogant is not the way for a good Muslim.
* We should not ridicule other people because of our differences with them.
* We should not make people with physical challenges feel small or insignificant.
* Mockery hurts the feelings of others and is not liked by Allāh ﷻ.

## EXERCISES

1. Give three reasons why people may be proud.
2. In the Qur'ān, *Surah* 31, verse 19, Allāh ﷻ says that a loud voice is like the braying of a _____
3. Give some examples of how people ridicule each other.
4. What are some of the reasons that people make fun of each other?
5. Why should we not mock and laugh at other people?
6. Describe what you would do to avoid mockery or stop others from mockery.
7. How should we treat the people who are physically chal lenged?

# LESSON 28

---

## EARNING A LIVING

### Honest Work

A mature, healthy Muslim should find work to support himself. He should not sit idle and expect others to support him. Rasūlullāh ﷺ said:

> *Never has anyone eaten a better thing than that*
> *which he eats from the work of his hand.*
> (Transmitted by Bukhāri)

The Qur'ān repeatedly emphasizes the importance of *'Amal as-Salih*, or good deeds. Every deed done with righteous intentions is like an act of worship and has a reward from Allāh ﷻ. A Muslim is taught to pray and work for the well being in both the worlds, *ad-Dunya* and *al-Akhirah*. The Qur'ān advises the believers:

وَٱبْتَغِ فِيمَآ ءَاتَىٰكَ ٱللَّهُ ٱلدَّارَ ٱلْأَخِرَةَ ۖ وَلَا تَنسَ نَصِيبَكَ مِنَ ٱلدُّنْيَا ۖ وَأَحْسِن كَمَآ أَحْسَنَ ٱللَّهُ إِلَيْكَ ۖ وَلَا تَبْغِ ٱلْفَسَادَ فِى ٱلْأَرْضِ ۖ إِنَّ ٱللَّهَ لَا يُحِبُّ ٱلْمُفْسِدِينَ ۞

*And seek, with the wealth that Allah has given you the home*
*of the Hereafter, nor forget your share in this world;*
*and be kind as Allah has been kind to you and seek not corruption*

*in the earth, for Allah loves not those who spread corruption.*
*(Al-Qasas 28:77)*

## Begging Is Not an Acceptable Way of Life

Rasūlullāh ﷺ is reported to have said:

*Whoever has food for a day and a night, it is forbidden for him to beg.*
(Transmitted by Abu Da'wud)

Rasūlullāh ﷺ never allowed his people to beg as a way of life. He always showed them how to earn their own living.

According to a *Ḥadīth* transmitted by Abu Da'wūd, a beggar from Madinah came to Rasūlullāh ﷺ. Rasūlullāh ﷺ asked him: "Have you nothing in your house?"

He replied: "Yes, I have woolen carpet, with part of which we cover ourselves and spread the rest. And I have a cup with which we drink water."

Rasūlullāh ﷺ said: "Come to me with them both."

The man came to him with them both, and Rasūlullāh ﷺ took them in his hand and said: "Who will buy these two?"

One man replied: "I will take them for one silver coin." repeating his offer several times.

Another man said: "I will take them for two silver coins."

Rasūlullāh ﷺ accepted this offer and took the two silver coins in exchange for the carpet and the cup. As he handed the two silver coins to the beggar, he advised: "Buy food for your family with one of these, and buy an axe with the other. Then, come to me with it."

So, the beggar did as Rasūlullāh ﷺ instructed. When he returned, Rasūlullāh ﷺ fixed a handle to the axe and instructed the beggar: "Go, cut wood, and sell it, and do not let me see you for fifteen days."

The man did as he was told. When he came back to Rasūlullāh ﷺ, he had earned ten silver coins. He was able to buy some clothes with and food with his wages.

Upon seeing him, Rasūlullāh ﷺ said: "This is better for you than if you were to come on the Day of Resurrection with black marks on your face."

## The Lessons of the *Ḥadīth*

The *Ḥadīth* quoted above teaches us many things. First of all, Rasūlullāh ﷺ did not approve of begging as a way of life for anyone who was capable of earning a living by working.

Second, just as Rasūlullāh ﷺ guided and helped the man to get started in his new work, we should also try to be helpful and offer constructive advice to someone in need. We should not just dismiss him as lazy and let him continue begging.

Finally, Rasūlullāh ﷺ informed us that on the Day of Resurrection, the beggars will have distinct scars and marks on the face that would disgrace them before others.

## Rasūlullāh ﷺ's Attitude Toward Poverty and Begging

Rasūlullāh ﷺ always cared for the poor. Even when he became the Head of State in Madinah, he lived a simple life. Sometimes, he and his family did not have enough to eat. Whenever they had something, they shared it with the poor, or gave it away as *Sadaqah* to others who were in need.

Islām established the payment of *Zakah* as a welfare tax, so that the Islāmic State could help people in need. Every Muslim should care for the welfare of those around him. Rasūlullāh ﷺ said:

> *He is not a Muslim who eats his fill while*
> *his neighbor goes hungry in his midst.*
> (Transmitted by Baihaqi)

Therefore, all Muslims, rich or poor, are urged to treat others with kindness and generosity. If everyone takes responsibility for his brothers and sisters, there will be no people deprived of food to eat. In fact, there will be no cause to beg and no excuse for those who make begging a way of life.

## WE HAVE LEARNED:

* A Muslim should work hard for both, this world and the Hereafter.
* Hard, honest work is one of the special traits of a good Muslim.
* If we find that we have run out of money, we should try our best to find other work and not beg or seek charity from others.

## EXERCISES

1. Which complies with the teaching of Islam, to beg or to find work?
2. Summarize the story of the man who came to beg from Rasūlullāh ﷺ
3. Think of two other ways to get to earn an honest living, in a village or a big town.
4. Complete the following *Ḥadīth*: ˝He is not a Muslim who eats

———————————————————— .

5. In light of this lesson, is it right for children to beg?

6. Describe the manner in which some children beg in a street and at Friday Mosques, and explain what you would do to discourage them and help them find a better way to earn money.

7. Think of two bad things that could happen to someone who is begging.

8. On the Day of Resurrection, how will the beggars be recognized?

9. Write a short essay explaining how do you plan to earn your living when you grow up.

# LESSON 29

---

## MODERATION IN LIVING

### A Muslim and Wealth

A Muslim should be moderate in his attitude toward wealth and possessions. One needs money for his own livelihood and the livelihood of his family, but money and possessions should not become his main interest and goal in life. If Allāh ﷻ blesses someone with wealth it must be used properly and shared with those people who are less fortunate. Allāh ﷻ reminds us in the Qur'ān:

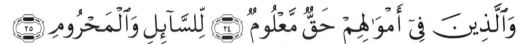

*And in their (Muslims) wealth there is a recognized*
*right for the needy and the poor.*
*(Al-Ma'arij 70:24-25)*

For some people, wealth becomes the most important thing in their lives. They care more for money than they care for truth, justice, kindness and respect for other people. They forget that misfortune or death may separate them from their wealth at any time and leave them with nothing.

A Muslim's goal in life, whether rich or poor, should be to faithfully serve Allāh ﷻ by obeying His commands and to seek His pleasure by being good to others. Rasūlullāh ﷺ makes this clear in this *Ḥadīth*:

> *He who seeks the world (wealth) in a lawful manner in order to*
> *avoid begging and to strive for (the maintenance of) his people,*
> *and for affection to his neighbor, shall meet Allah on the Day of*

*Resurrection with his face (shining) like a moon; and he who seeks*
*the world (wealth) in an unlawful manner, for pride and show,*
*shall meet Allah and He will be angry with him.*
(Transmitted by Baihaqi)

## Wastefulness

A Muslim should not use his wealth on useless things in a wasteful manner. If he has more money than he can reasonably use on necessary things, he should give it to a useful cause rather than waste it. He should spend his wealth in a manner that will earn him a good reward from Allāh ﷻ in the Hereafter.

Rasūlullāh ﷺ said:

*Truly Allah hates three things in you: quarreling,*
*wasting one's wealth, and frequent, useless questions.*
(Transmitted by Bukhari and Muslim)

## Generosity vs. Stinginess

A Muslim should be generous and hospitable, ready to share whatever he has. However, he should not give away so freely that he finds himself in need. He should keep enough for himself to provide the reasonable needs of his family. Taking care of the family needs is a vital responsibility for a believer. He should also try to leave behind enough, so that they are not reduced to poverty.

Allāh ﷻ says in the Qur'ān:

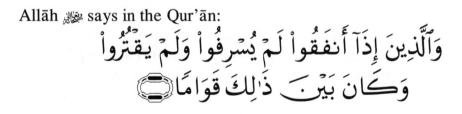

108

*(The faithful servants of Allah the Beneficent are) those who,
when they spend, are not extravagant and not stingy,
but hold a just (balance) between those (extremes).*
*(Al-Furqan 25:67)*

Again, the emphasis is on moderation. Going to extremes in any case is never good. In another verse, Allāh ﷻ says:

$$\text{وَلَا تَجْعَلْ يَدَكَ مَغْلُولَةً إِلَىٰ عُنُقِكَ وَلَا تَبْسُطْهَا كُلَّ ٱلْبَسْطِ}$$

$$\text{فَتَقْعُدَ مَلُومًا مَّحْسُورًا ۝}$$

*And make not your hand tied to neck, nor stretch it forth to its
utmost reach, so that you become blameworthy and destitute.*
*(Al-Isra' 17:29)*

While a Muslim should avoid stinginess, he should also be cautious of extravagant indulgences at the expense of his own obligations. Allāh ﷻ loves generosity, but taking care of one's family obligations come first. The main idea of Islam is to keep a balanced life and avoid the extremes.

## WE HAVE LEARNED:

* A Muslim should live a simple and modest life, following the example of Rasūlullāh ﷺ.
* Our wealth is a gift from Allāh ﷻ and therefore must not be wasted.
* Generosity is a good habit to develop.

## EXERCISES

1. What is the real use of wealth?
2. What is the aim of Muslim's life?
3. What is the danger of making wealth the primary aim of one's life?

4.   What should a Muslim do with any extra wealth beyond his needs?

5.   Why is it better for a Muslim to spend his wealth to earn a good reward from Allāh ﷻ rather than waste wealth in this life?

6.   Describe three instances in which people tend to waste money. Describe what you would do in each instance to avoid wastefulness.

7.   Describe three different ways in which you can show gen erosity or hospitality to others, with or without spending money.

# LESSON 30

## GAMBLING

### What is Gambling?

Gambling means to wager money or anything else on the chance win of some event. People usually gamble because they want to make a lot of money quickly without any real effort. They may bet on a game of cards, horse-racing, football games, the lottery, or on any other activity. People also gamble in casinos organized by big commercial companies. Sometimes, they win, but most of the time, they lose. The real winners are the casino owners, who take part of every win, and the government, who benefits by taking part of the profit as taxes. Many people consider gambling a form of entertainment, but as we will see in this lesson, gambling has dangerous consequences.

### Allah's Prohibition of Gambling

Allāh ﷻ says in the Qur'ān:

$$\text{يَـٰٓأَيُّهَا ٱلَّذِينَ ءَامَنُوٓاْ إِنَّمَا ٱلۡخَمۡرُ وَٱلۡمَيۡسِرُ وَٱلۡأَنصَابُ وَٱلۡأَزۡلَـٰمُ رِجۡسٌ مِّنۡ عَمَلِ ٱلشَّيۡطَـٰنِ فَٱجۡتَنِبُوهُ لَعَلَّكُمۡ تُفۡلِحُونَ}$$

*O you who believe! Intoxicants and games of chance (gambling) and idolatrous practices and foretelling the future are but a loathsome evil*

111

*of Satan's doing; avoid it, then, so that you may be graced with good ever-
lasting.*
*(Al-Ma'idah 5:90)*

Along with intoxication, *kufr* (disbelief), and fortune telling, gambling is
one of the most clearly prohibited acts in the Qur'ān. All these prohibitions serve our well being, and as Muslims, we are not only advised but
also bound to abstain from them. The Qur'ān describes them correctly the
works of *Shaitān*:

إِنَّمَا يُرِيدُ ٱلشَّيْطَـٰنُ أَن يُوقِعَ بَيْنَكُمُ ٱلْعَدَٰوَةَ وَٱلْبَغْضَآءَ فِى
ٱلْخَمْرِ وَٱلْمَيْسِرِ وَيَصُدَّكُمْ عَن ذِكْرِ ٱللَّهِ وَعَنِ ٱلصَّلَوٰةِ
فَهَلْ أَنتُم مُّنتَهُونَ ۝

*By means of intoxicants and gambling, Satan seeks only to sow
enmity and hatred among you and turn you away from the
remembrance to Allah and from the prayer.
Will you not from them desist?*
*(Al-Ma'idah 5:91)*

It is obvious that gambling is strictly forbidden in Islam. The *Shaitān* uses
the temptation of gambling to lure people away from worship and develop
animosity among believers.

## What is the Harm of Gambling?

Gambling can become an addictive habit. When a person gambles, he
becomes so absorbed that he forgets all his obligations. The first time, he
may win, but eventually, he is bound to lose. Still, he keeps making
wagers in the hope that he may win back all that he has lost. Finally, he

bets away everything he owns, resulting in debts and bankruptcy. Sometimes, a gambler may even steal in order to continue his habit. Not only does he lose all his money, he loses his family's respect, his friends, and his own self-respect, and above all, he loses Allāh ﷻ's protection and guidance.

Allāh ﷻ forbids all forms of gambling. To avoid temptation, a Muslim should refrain from watching gambling.

Gambling has become a real problem, especially in western societies. Many people face financial and personal ruin, because their gambling is so out of control. Some even become suicidal. Counselors and support groups, like Gamblers Anonymous, try to help chronic gamblers and try to help them control their addiction. Islam has given us a code of life that prevents such addiction and keeps our body, mind and spirit healthy.

## WE HAVE LEARNED:

* Gambling is absolutely forbidden in Islam.
* The *Shaitān* makes us think that gambling is a fun way to make fast money.
* Gambling can ruin a person, spiritually, socially, and financially.

### EXERCISES

1. What is gambling? Give some examples of gambling.
2. Describe some evils of gambling?
3. Who really profits from casino gambling?
4. Describe the measures you would take to avoid the temptation of gambling.

# LESSON 31

## BRIBERY AND CORRUPTION

### What are Bribery and Corruption?

Bribery and corruption refer to the giving and receiving of gifts in return for undue favors. This should not, however, be confused with giving gifts out of love and respect.

Let's take the next few examples:

### Example No. 1:
A builder wants to win a contract. Several others are applying for the same contract, so the contractor visits the members of the City Council and gives money to some influential members. As a result, they favor him, and he wins the contract.

### Example No. 2:
A driver is caught by the police for drunken driving. The policeman takes his name and vehicle number to give him a ticket. The driver gives him some money (a bribe), and the policeman lets him go.

### Example No. 3:
A rich businessman builds a factory on someone's land. The owner of the land takes him to court. The businessman bribes the judge, and the judge decides that the land belongs to the businessman.

In all three examples, we see that someone gets an unfair advantage by bribing someone in authority. In all three cases, the party who gives the bribe and the party who takes the bribe are guilty of corruption. According to a *Hadith* transmitted by At-Tirmidhi, Rasūlullāh ﷺ denounced the giver and the taker of bribes.

Allāh ﷻ has condemned such dishonest practices in the Qur'ān:

وَلَا تَأْكُلُوٓاْ أَمْوَٰلَكُم بَيْنَكُم بِٱلْبَٰطِلِ وَتُدْلُواْ بِهَآ إِلَى ٱلْحُكَّامِ لِتَأْكُلُواْ فَرِيقًا مِّنْ أَمْوَٰلِ ٱلنَّاسِ بِٱلْإِثْمِ وَأَنتُمْ تَعْلَمُونَ ۞

*And do not eat up your property among yourselves for vanities, nor use it as bait for the judges, with the intent that you may eat up wrongfully and knowingly a little of (other) people's property.*
(*Al-Baqarah 2:188*)

## What is the Harm of Bribery and Corruption?

Corruption and bribery begin when people are not satisfied with their salaries. They become greedy and want more money. They refuse to do even their designated duties, unless they are bribed. Rasūlullāh ﷺ is reported to have said of such corrupt officials:

*If he whom we have appointed as a salaried official takes anything above his salary he is a wrong-doer.*
(Transmitted by Abū Da'wūd)

There are many reasons why bribery and corruption are wrong. First of all, no one is treated fairly. The rights of the poor are often neglected or violated, because they have no money for bribes. Similarly, the rights of honest people are often withheld, because they refuse to give bribes. There is no respect for right and wrong, and no respect for the law - only respect for money.

Second, the balance of the economy is disrupted. The rich get richer, and the poor get poorer, creating divisions of hatred and fear among the socioeconomic classes. Therefore, the cost of everything goes up. People spend more and more money and get fewer benefits. The nation's economy weakens and eventually collapses.

## The Shame of Bribery and Corruption

Bribery and corruption are a matter of great shame in this world and the Hereafter. Money or other things received as bribes are *Harām* (forbidden) and can never be a source of good. There is no *Barakah* in wealth gained through corruption. *Akl halāl* (rightful earnings) are very important in Islām. A *Halāl* earning comes from honest, hard work in a lawful occupation. We will discuss the value of work and the distinctions that define *Halāl* and *Harām* occupations.

Often, people try to mask bribery by calling it a gift or a favor. According to their view, it is merely an act of appreciation for special treatment of help, and after all, no one gets hurt. They are wrong in thinking no one gets hurt; the people who don't offer bribes are being cheated out of a fair chance for equal treatment. Such people only deceive themselves by making such false justifications for their wrongdoing, because Allāh ﷻ knows what is really in their hearts.

To the contrary, a Muslim knows that the word of Allāh ﷻ and His Messenger s is true and must be followed. He knows that there is no *Barakah* in wealth earned unlawfully. *Barakah* is the power to provide for all our needs and desires in a way that is most beneficial to us. Only Allāh ﷻ can give *Barakah* to our earnings, and when angered, He can take it away. If not by plentiful earnings, *Barakah* comes in the form of good health, good family and friends, without whom any amount of wealth would be meaningless.

A Muslim should uphold justice and the truth and refuse to give or receive bribes. A Muslim should not ruin his honor and good name for material gain. He should not incur the anger of Allāh ﷻ because of selfish greed and ingratitude to his Lord.

## WE HAVE LEARNED:

* Bribery and corruption destroy our own peace of mind and lead societies to their downfall.
* Every corrupt person tries to justify his/her misguided deeds, but a Muslim must follow the Qur'ān and the *Sunnah* and avoid all forbidden acts.
* A Muslim must be honorable in all situations and should not offer nor accept bribes.

## EXERCISES

1. Give some examples of bribery and corruption.
2. Explain three harmful effects of bribery and corruption.
3. What does the Qur'ān say about bribery and corruption?
4. Rasūlullāh ﷺ says that a judge who accepts a bribe is guilty of *"kufr."* Explain the meaning of *"kufr"* and why the guilt of bribery merits this description.
5. Why should a Muslim avoid bribery and corruption? (Give two reasons)
6. What does *Barakah* mean? What does it mean to lose the *Barakah*.

# LESSON 32

## STEALING

### Why do People Steal?

People steal because they want or need something without having to pay for it. They forcefully take it from its rightful owner or sneak it away without the owner's knowledge. Some people are more aggressive; they break into people's homes, businesses and property and commit thefts. Yet, some thieves resort to violence, often harming or killing the people they rob.

Islām grants every human being the right to his money, property and personal possessions. Personal property belongs to the owner because he earned it by working or he received it as a gift. If the owner consents, we may purchase his property at an agreed upon price. But no one has the right to steal to satisfy his own greed.

### The Needs of the Poor

While Islām establishes strict rules for the defense of private property and prescribes severe punishments for those who violate them, it does require the community to develop a welfare system in which the basic needs of every individual are met, so that no one is left without proper care. While the Muslim owner has the right to his lawful property, he does have two duties towards the poor. One duty is to pay the *Zakah* (Welfare Tax) on his savings and property, for the care of the poor, the needy, debtors, stranded travelers, and others in difficulties. The *Zakah* is compulsory if a person's wealth or property has reached a certain fixed value known as *Nisab*.

The second duty of a Muslim is to be aware of the needs of those around him, such as relatives, neighbors, co-workers and friends. Helping them meet their needs is an Islāmic obligation. This kind of giving is called *Hadiyyah,* or a gift.

Sometimes, the needs of society cannot be met by the *Zakah* or *Hadiyyah* alone. This is why *Sadaqah*, or charity, is encouraged. *Sadaqah* is voluntary gift giving or helping those in need.

Therefore, both the State and the Muslims individually have a duty to help the needy. Many times people steal because of their needs. Later it may become their habit. They may come to the idea that if the state or community is not taking care of their needs they are justified in stealing. Wrong thoughts lead to wrong actions and wrong actions destroy good moral values of the society.

## Stealing and its Punishment

Most cases of theft come from greed and not need. The thief wants something, but he does not want to work for it, so he steals. For such thieves, the law of Islām (the *Sharī'ah*) is specifically strict. Allāh ﷻ says in the Qur'ān:

وَٱلسَّارِقُ وَٱلسَّارِقَةُ فَٱقْطَعُوٓاْ أَيْدِيَهُمَا جَزَآءً بِمَا كَسَبَا نَكَٰلًا مِّنَ ٱللَّهِ ۗ

*As to the thief, male or female, cut off his or her hands: a retribution for their deed and exemplary punishment from Allāh.....*
*(Al-Ma'idah 5:38)*

Before handing down his judgment, a judge should examine the motive and circumstances surrounding the theft. If the person was hungry or des-

119

perately needy, the judge may show leniency and prescribe a lesser punishment. If he sees true regret for the action, he may release the offender with a warning. The judge may also instruct the Islāmic State to train him for some useful occupation or provide his needs until he is able to do so himself.

## The Effectiveness of *Sharī'ah* in Preventing Stealing

The severe punishment of the *Sharī'ah* for stealing is enough to stop almost anyone from stealing. As a result, stealing is almost unknown in countries where the *Sharī'ah* is applied. People are safe from robbers. They even leave their shops unlocked and unprotected when they go for prayers. Even property found in the street or left on buses is not stolen. The owner will almost always be able to find it, if he can remember where he left it.

So, the *Sharī'ah* punishment for stealing protects the property of innocent people who earn an honest living, and people are safe from the fear of robbers and thieves.

## WE HAVE LEARNED:

* No one has the right to steal or forcefully take something that belongs to another person.
* The Muslim state, Muslim community and Muslim individual have a special responsibility to take care of the needs of every member of society.
* The *Sharī'ah* is the Islāmic law that serves to safeguard the interests of society.

## EXERCISES

1.     Why does the owner have a right to his property?

120

2. How the needs of the poor and needy must be met by:
   (a) The Islāmic State?
   (b) Muslim Community
   (b) The individual Muslim?
3. What is the punishment under the *Sharī'ah* (Islāmic Law) for stealing?
4. How would a Muslim *Qadi*, judge, apply *Sharī'ah* in case of stealing?
5. How do we know the *Sharī'ah* punishment for stealing is effective?
6. Read the newspapers for one week, and write a report about the situation of crime in your society?
7. Write an argumentative essay in favor or against severe punishment.

# LESSON 33

## CHEATING

### Cheating is Similar to Stealing

Cheating means to commit a fraud or take something deceitfully that belongs to someone else. In the last lesson, we learned about stealing and its punishment. Cheating is similar, but while stealing is an obvious deception, cheating is not as easy to catch. A person who cheats very often does not even think he is doing something wrong. There are so many ways of cheating and, unfortunately, some of them have become social norms. Let us take a look at some of the way people cheat.

### Cheating on Tests

A youth may cheat on tests by copying answers from other students or by hiding a book under the desk. If he is not caught, he may get high marks and snatch the top position in the class from another youth who had studied hard and deserved better. Like a thief, he hopes to get something for nothing.

### Cheating in Trade

In regards to trade practices, Rasūlullāh ﷺ said that when a vendor does not tell the truth about what he is selling, he is cheating the customer. Sometimes, a trader cheats by changing his weights and measures so that the customer gets less than he pays for. He may tell the buyer that it is in perfect condition, when it really has something wrong with it. Rasūlullāh ﷺ's warned merchants and businessmen:

The merchants will be raised on the Day of Judgment as evildoers except those who fear Allāh ﷻ, are honest and speak the truth.
(Transmitted by Tirmidhi, Ibn Majah, and Darimi)

Often, merchants charge the customer for a high quality product but deliver a lower and cheaper quality. On one specific occasion during Rasūlullāh ﷺ's lifetime, a man displayed some goods in the market. In an effort to wheedle more money out of his customer, he falsely told him that he had already been offered a higher price for the goods. On that occasion this verse was revealed:

$$ إِنَّ ٱلَّذِينَ يَشْتَرُونَ بِعَهْدِ ٱللَّهِ وَأَيْمَٰنِهِمْ ثَمَنًا قَلِيلًا $$

$$ أُوْلَٰٓئِكَ لَا خَلَٰقَ لَهُمْ فِى ٱلْأَخِرَةِ $$

*Verily! Those who purchase a small gain at the cost of*
*Allāh's Covenant and their oaths shall have no portion in the Hereafter.*
(Āli 'Imrān 3:77)

## Cheating at the Workplace

Another form of cheating is very common among office workers and others who are paid a monthly salary. When they arrive late, leave early, and go to another office and chat instead of doing their work, they cheat their employers. In case of government employees the cheating of affects the entire society.

Yet, if their employers decided not to pay their dues because of their failure to complete their work, they would be angry. They feel that their full salary is a right, whether they work properly or not. That is the wrong attitude and is very un-Islāmic.

## What the Qur'ān Says About Cheating

Allāh ﷻ enjoins upon us to be judicious in all affairs. A believer must be fair to everyone.

وَزِنُواْ بِٱلْقِسْطَاسِ ٱلْمُسْتَقِيمِ ۝ وَلَا تَبْخَسُواْ ٱلنَّاسَ أَشْيَاءَهُمْ وَلَا تَعْثَوْاْ فِى ٱلْأَرْضِ مُفْسِدِينَ ۝ وَٱتَّقُواْ ٱلَّذِى خَلَقَكُمْ وَٱلْجِبِلَّةَ ٱلْأَوَّلِينَ ۝

*And weigh with scales true and upright.*
*And withhold not things justly due to men,*
*nor do evil in the land, working mischief.*
*And fear Him Who created you and the generations before (you).*
*(Ash-Shu'ara 26: 182-4)*

The Qur'ān condemns those who are dishonest and gives them strong warning of punishment:

وَيْلٌ لِّلْمُطَفِّفِينَ ۝ ٱلَّذِينَ إِذَا ٱكْتَالُواْ عَلَى ٱلنَّاسِ يَسْتَوْفُونَ ۝ وَإِذَا كَالُوهُمْ أَو وَّزَنُوهُمْ يُخْسِرُونَ ۝ أَلَا يَظُنُّ أُوْلَـٰئِكَ أَنَّهُم مَّبْعُوثُونَ ۝ لِيَوْمٍ عَظِيمٍ ۝ يَوْمَ يَقُومُ ٱلنَّاسُ لِرَبِّ ٱلْعَـٰلَمِينَ ۝

*Woe to those that deal in fraud - those who, when they have to*

124

*receive by measure from people, exact full measure, but when*
*they have to give by measure or weight to men, give less than due.*
*Do they not think that they will be raised up on a Mighty Day,*
*a Day when (all) mankind will stand before the Lord of the Worlds?*
*(Al-Mutaffifin 83:1-6)*

## WE HAVE LEARNED:

* Cheating is like stealing, except that it is harder to catch.
* Allāh ﷻ wants the Muslims to be judicious.
* People who cheat eventually get caught, if not in this life, then in the next.

## EXERCISES

1. How is cheating like stealing?
2. Why is it wrong to cheat on tests?
3. How do some people cheat in trade?
4. How do some people cheat at the workplace?
5. What are various other ways in which people cheat?
6. Explain in your own words what the Qur'ān says about cheating.
7. In some American colleges students are provided with take-home examinations. The college expects students not to cheat. Is this system practical for your school? Why or why not?

# LESSON 34

---

## ALCOHOL, ILLICIT DRUGS AND SMOKING

### What is Alcohol?

Alcoholic drinks and other artificial stimulants can cause a person to lose all sense of reality. Under the influence of such substances, one's understanding of right and wrong become distorted. He loses control over his mind and body.

There are all kinds of alcoholic drinks, such as beer, wine, whisky, gin, brandy, vodka and so on. In most societies, they are sold freely through special stores and served in bars. Unfortunately, most Muslim countries wrongfully permit the legal sale of alcohol. Students should lobby through letter-writing campaigns for the prohibition of alcohol and other illicit drugs.

### What are Illicit Drugs?

Illicit drugs are substances - herbs, pills, capsules or powders - that can cause a person to behave in a strange manner. Just like alcohol, they cause a person to lose touch with reality. Examples of illicit drugs are marijuana, heroine, cocaine, and certain tablets or capsules that can cause a person to be either very alert or very sleepy, and see or hear things which are not really there. In most countries, these substances are illegal, but a few countries do allow them. In countries where they are illegal, the punishments are severe for drug dealers and users.

# What is the Harm of Alcohol and Dangerous Drugs?

There are many dangers of alcohol and drugs. They poison the body, confuse the brain and cause early death. Because they are addictive, the person taking them wants them more and more, until he finds that he cannot live without them. Some addicts would lie, steal, or even kill to satisfy their addiction.

Most of the time, drugs and alcohol cause people to lose control over their behavior. They may even become violent and hurt others as well as themselves. Alcohol and drugs cause the break-up of families because of the unreasonable and often violent behavior of the person who is taking them.

Addiction to alcohol is called alcoholism. Alcoholism is a disease that often results in liver damage or even death. An increasingly prevalent problem in the West, many hospitals, clinics, and services such as Alcoholics Anonymous have had some success in helping people control their addiction.

Drunk driving is one of the perils of alcoholism. Drunk drivers not only endanger their own lives but also jeopardize the lives of the others. It is especially a problem on certain holidays. After drinking and partying, they drive carelessly and cause often fatal accidents. Thousands of innocent lives are lost each year because of their actions.

Muslims are clearly forbidden from intoxication in the Qur'ān. In fact, it is one of the major evils condemned by Allāh ﷻ in the Qur'ān:

يَـٰٓأَيُّهَا ٱلَّذِينَ ءَامَنُوٓاْ إِنَّمَا ٱلۡخَمۡرُ وَٱلۡمَيۡسِرُ وَٱلۡأَنصَابُ وَٱلۡأَزۡلَـٰمُ رِجۡسٌ مِّنۡ عَمَلِ ٱلشَّيۡطَـٰنِ فَٱجۡتَنِبُوهُ لَعَلَّكُمۡ تُفۡلِحُونَ ۝ إِنَّمَا يُرِيدُ ٱلشَّيۡطَـٰنُ أَن يُوقِعَ بَيۡنَكُمۡ

127

$$\text{ٱلْعَدَاوَةَ وَٱلْبَغْضَاءَ فِى ٱلْخَمْرِ وَٱلْمَيْسِرِ وَيَصُدَّكُمْ عَن ذِكْرِ}$$

$$\text{ٱللَّهِ وَعَنِ ٱلصَّلَوٰةِ ۖ فَهَلْ أَنتُم مُّنتَهُونَ ۝}$$

*O you who believe! <u>Khamr</u> (alcohol and intoxicating drugs) and
gambling and idolatrous practices and foretelling the future are but
a hateful evil of Satan's doing; therefore, shun it, so that you may
be raised with good everlasting. By means of <u>Khamr</u> and gambling,
Satan seeks only to sow enmity and hatred among you and turn you
away from the remembrance of Allāh and from prayer.
Will you not then desist?
(Al-Ma'idah 5:90-91)*

Unfortunately, despite Allāh's injunctions against it, some misguided
Muslims do drink and even use drugs. Consequently, they begin to forget
Allāh ﷻ, forget their prayers, and forget the difference between right and
wrong. Their lives become dangerously reckless. They mistreat their families and neglect their responsibilities. It works like a slow poison, infect-
ing their entire being. For this reason, Allāh ﷻ curses anyone who makes,
buys, sells, stores or carries <u>Khamr</u>. Rasūlullāh ﷺ aptly describes the evils
linked to it in the following <u>Hadīth</u>:

*Do not use <u>Khamr</u>. Its evil effects give rise to many evils in the
same way as a tree trunk multiplies into many branches.*
(Transmitted by Ibn Majah)

According to another *Hadīth*, <u>Khamr</u> is prohibited in even small amounts,
further emphasizing the potency of its dangers. These prohibitions are
truly a sign of Allāh's Mercy, because they serve to protect us from our
own natural human weaknesses. Without His warnings, we would not
know the dangers of <u>Khamr</u> without having experienced them.

128

# Avoiding *Khamr*

Sometimes, people try to convince us to do things we know are wrong. As teenagers, many students like to experiment with new things, trying to develop their own identity. However, we must remember to stay within the boundaries Islām has set for us. Sometimes, young people feel pressured to try alcohol or drugs in order to be accepted by their peers. It is important to remember that your commitment to Allāh ﷻ comes before everything else. If you remain true to Him, He will provide you friends who do not need alcohol to enjoy themselves.

Sometimes, students take artificial stimulants to stay awake at night and study for examinations. These drugs, if prescribed by a doctor and used accordingly, do not fall under the same prohibitive category as other intoxicants. However, if they are abused and become addictive, causing the user to lose touch with reality, then they will be considered *Harām*. A Muslim student should know that the mind and body need rest. Fresh *Wuḍū'* and *Ṣalāh* are better alternatives to keep awake and relaxed than artificial stimulants. Academic success comes from organizing one's study habits and trusting that no matter what the result of the exam, Allāh ﷻ knows best.

# Smoking

Smoking is bad for the health. It fills the lungs with tar. It can cause diseases of the lungs, such as emphysema and lung cancer. It is unhealthy for the smoker as well as for those around him.

Just like alcoholism, smoking is addictive. The person who smokes always wants to smoke more and finds it every difficult to stop. Smoking gives the body and breath a bad odor. It is a waste of money, as it has no benefit at all. It is now proven that both smoking and secondary smoke (being in the presence of a person when he/she smokes) contribute to cancer and several lung diseases. It is now mandatory that all cigarette packets and advertisements carry a warning against the hazards of smoking.

According to some *Fuqaha'*, smoking is also forbidden in Islām. They argue their case on the basis of the following verse of the Qur'ān:

وَأَنفِقُوا۟ فِى سَبِيلِ ٱللَّهِ وَلَا تُلْقُوا۟ بِأَيْدِيكُمْ إِلَى ٱلتَّهْلُكَةِ وَأَحْسِنُوٓا۟ إِنَّ ٱللَّهَ يُحِبُّ ٱلْمُحْسِنِينَ ۝

*.... and make not your own hands contribute to (your) destruction,*
*but do good; for Allāh loves those who do good.*
(*Al-Baqarah* 2:195)

The argument is that a Muslim should not destroy his health with his own hands by taking a cigarette.

## WE HAVE LEARNED:

* Our health is a gift from Allāh ﷻ, and we must not abuse it.
* Alcohol, drugs and cigarettes are injurious to our bodies and souls.
* Dealing in any way with these harmful substances is *Harām*.

## EXERCISES

1. How does *Khamr* (intoxicants) affect a person's behavior, the body and brain?
2. What is meant by "addictive"?
3. How does *Khamr* affect the family of the person who is addicted?
4. Why are Muslims not allowed to take even a small amount of *Khamr*?
5. "*Khamr* is the beginning of many evils." Explain what this means.
6. Why should a Muslim avoid smoking?

# LESSON 35

## THE DANGERS OF FORTUNE-TELLING

### What are Fortune-tellers and Psychics?

Fortune-tellers are people who claim to be able to see what will happen to a person in the future, or what has happened to him in the past. They claim to predict the future by various means: reading palms, marking lines in the sand or studying the intestines of dead animals, looking at cards, or reading patterns in tea leaves, etc. Many of them claim to have connections to the spirit world.

### Rasūlullāh ﷺ Prohibited Going to Fortune-tellers and Psychics

According to a *Hadīth* related by Muslim, one *Ṣahabi* of Rasūlullāh ﷺ pointed out, "Among us are some men who go to consult the fortune-tellers." Rasūlullāh ﷺ replied, "Then, do not go to them."

According to another *Hadīth* related by Muslim, Rasūlullāh ﷺ also warned against allowing fortune-tellers to affect our decisions.

Islām teaches us that no one knows the future except Allāh ﷻ, and no one controls the future events except Him. Therefore, consulting fortune-tellers and psychics in the hope of finding out about one's future is forbidden in Islām. By doing so, we are putting our trust in others than Allāh ﷻ. This consultation and reliance on their advice can be considered an act of *Shirk* (associating someone with the Power of Allāh ﷻ). *Shirk* is among the acts most hated by Allāh ﷻ.

Therefore, one should avoid going to astrologers, psychics, or fortune-tellers. One should have faith only in Allāh ﷻ and trust Him for the future.

## What is the Harm in Listening to Fortune-Tellers and Psychics?

Some people seek a fortune-teller's advice about what to do and what not to do instead of following their own logic and common sense and trusting in Allāh ﷻ. The fortune-teller becomes like a god to them - he tells them when they should travel, when they should move, when they should get married, and so on. They cannot decide anything for themselves and do not rely on Allāh ﷻ.

The fortune-teller can take advantage of people by making them believe he has special powers by creating deceptive illusions. He takes their money and wastes their time. Even worse, he diminishes their faith and self-confidence.

Allāh ﷻ has given us eyes, ears, a tongue, as well as consciousness of right and wrong, common sense, reason and wisdom. He has also given us the Qur'ān as guidance. These are the tools we should use to decide what to do and when to do it. We should not depend entirely on another human being who may be right or wrong, even if he does claim to see into the future.

Only Allāh ﷻ knows the future. Sometimes, we find ourselves in difficult circumstances. Such times are a test from Allāh ﷻ. If we are faithful and turn to Him for help, He will guide us through to better times. If we become impatient and start looking for answers elsewhere, we will lose His guidance and never find our way out. We learn from the Qur'ān:

وَلَنَبْلُوَنَّكُم بِشَىْءٍ مِّنَ ٱلْخَوْفِ وَٱلْجُوعِ وَنَقْصٍ مِّنَ ٱلْأَمْوَٰلِ وَٱلْأَنفُسِ وَٱلثَّمَرَٰتِ ۗ وَبَشِّرِ ٱلصَّٰبِرِينَ ۝

*Be sure we shall test you with something of fear and hunger, some*
*loss in goods, lives, and the fruits (of your toil), but give glad tidings to*
*those who patiently persevere....*
*(Al-Baqarah 2:155)*

Now, we completely understand the verse from *Sūrah Ma'idah* warning us
against the *Shaitān's* evil:

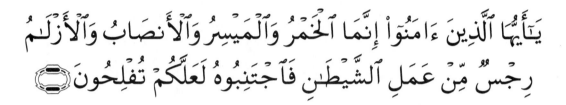

*O you who believe! Khamr (alcohol and intoxicating drugs)*
*and gambling and idolatrous practices and foretelling the future*
*are but a hateful evil of Satan's doing; therefore, shun it,*
*so that you may be raised with good everlasting.*
*(Al-Ma'idah 5: 90)*

## WE HAVE LEARNED:

* Rasūlullāh ﷺ warned us to stay away from psychics and
  fortune-tellers.
* Only Allāh ﷻ ultimately decides what happens in our future.
* What ever happens in our lives, good or bad, comes from the Will
  of Allāh ﷻ.

## EXERCISES

1.  Give some examples of how fortune-tellers claim to predict
    the future.
2.  What did Rasūlullāh ﷺ say about going to a fortune-teller?

3. What tools from Allāh ﷻ should a Muslim use as his guide in deciding what to do and when to do it?
4. Describe three circumstances under which some people go to fortune-tellers.
5. Why should a Muslim trust Allāh ﷻ all the time?
6. What does the putting of our faith in the fortune-tellers do to us?

# LESSON 36

---

## CHASTITY

### Modesty of Dress and Behavior

In Lesson 13, we learned that a Muslim should be modest. Whether a boy or a girl, he/she should dress modestly and follow the Islāmic dress code. Whether in mixed company or with company of the same sex, men and women must observe the rules of modesty.

Relationships between men and women can be very complex. While simple friendships may seem harmless, they can often lead to immoral behavior. For this reason, Islām does not allow free mingling of the sexes or any intimate relationship between men and women outside marriage.

In *Surah An-Nūr,* the Qur'ān has specifically addressed this issue in regards to the behavior of men and women. For men, it advises:

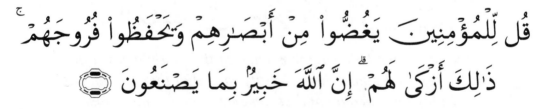

*Say to the believing men, that they should
lower their gaze and guard their chastity.
That will make great purity for them: and Allāh
is well acquainted with all they do.*
(An-Nur 24:30)

Then, it addresses women:

وَقُل لِّلْمُؤْمِنَٰتِ يَغْضُضْنَ مِنْ أَبْصَٰرِهِنَّ وَيَحْفَظْنَ فُرُوجَهُنَّ وَلَا يُبْدِينَ زِينَتَهُنَّ إِلَّا مَا ظَهَرَ مِنْهَا ۖ وَلْيَضْرِبْنَ بِخُمُرِهِنَّ عَلَىٰ جُيُوبِهِنَّ ۖ وَلَا يُبْدِينَ زِينَتَهُنَّ إِلَّا لِبُعُولَتِهِنَّ أَوْ ءَابَآئِهِنَّ أَوْ ءَابَآءِ بُعُولَتِهِنَّ أَوْ أَبْنَآئِهِنَّ أَوْ أَبْنَآءِ بُعُولَتِهِنَّ أَوْ إِخْوَٰنِهِنَّ أَوْ بَنِىٓ إِخْوَٰنِهِنَّ أَوْ بَنِىٓ أَخَوَٰتِهِنَّ أَوْ نِسَآئِهِنَّ أَوْ مَا مَلَكَتْ أَيْمَٰنُهُنَّ أَوِ ٱلتَّٰبِعِينَ غَيْرِ أُو۟لِى ٱلْإِرْبَةِ مِنَ ٱلرِّجَالِ أَوِ ٱلطِّفْلِ ٱلَّذِينَ لَمْ يَظْهَرُوا۟ عَلَىٰ عَوْرَٰتِ ٱلنِّسَآءِ ۖ وَلَا يَضْرِبْنَ بِأَرْجُلِهِنَّ لِيُعْلَمَ مَا يُخْفِينَ مِن زِينَتِهِنَّ ۚ وَتُوبُوٓا۟ إِلَى ٱللَّهِ جَمِيعًا أَيُّهَ ٱلْمُؤْمِنُونَ لَعَلَّكُمْ تُفْلِحُونَ ۝

*And say to the believing women, that they should restrain their eyes, and guard their chastity; and that they should not display their beauty and ornaments, except what (must ordinarily) appears of them.  And that they draw their veils over their bosoms and display not their beauty except to their husbands, or their fathers, or their sons, or their husband's sons, or their brothers, or their brother's sons, or their sister's sons, or their women, or their slaves, or male domestics who have no natural sexual force, or children who know nothing of women's nakedness.  And let them not strike*

*their feet together so as to reveal their hidden ornaments. And*
*repent you all to Allāh, O you believers, that you may succeed.*
(*An-Nur* 24:31)

In other places, the Qur'ān has made exceptions for close relations such as husbands, fathers, sons, their brothers and old servants etc. Note the emphasis on lowering the gaze for both men and women. Often, Shaitān uses our own senses to distract and mislead us, especially our eyes. Additionally, women are especially warned to guard themselves against the desires of men. Allāh ﷻ created both men and women with certain weaknesses, of which only He has the best knowledge. On the basis of His perfect knowledge, He has ordained these rules for our own well being and protection. As true believers, we must accept and submit to this fact. If we think about it carefully, doing so is indeed in our best interest.

## Islām does not Approve Dating

The western tradition of dating is forbidden in Islām. Muslim boys are not allowed to go out with girls before marriage, and Muslim girls are not allowed to go out with boys before marriage. Aside from blood ties, the only relationship between the opposite sexes approved by Islām is marriage. Dating is not approved in Islām, because it leads to unlawful intimacy between men and women.

People argue that without dating, you cannot get to know someone well enough to marry them. However, in reality, it is not the best way to see a person for whom they really are. When two people are dating, they put forth their best behavior to impress the other person. Often, people hide their true personalities in their effort to keep the other person satisfied, so he/she won't leave them. However, when they get married, they may be disappointed by the real personality of their spouse, which only comes out after they have started living together as husband and wife.

# Chastity Before Marriage

A Muslim boy and girl should be chaste before marriage.  The natural attraction between the opposite sexes is one of Allāh ﷻ's tests of faith. By avoiding being alone together, boys and girls can prevent temptation. There is a well-known *Hadīth*: that says:

> *Whenever a man is alone with a woman, Shaitān is the third (present).*
> (Transmitted by Tirmidhi)

This is why Islām does not approve of the free mixing of men and women who are not married to each other or closely related by blood.  At the work-place or at school, where men and women have no choice but to work together, they should be reserved, maintaining a physical distance with each other and lowering their gaze while limiting conversations to business or academic matters only.

In the West, where women are professed to be the most liberated in the world, demeaning comments and physical advances by male colleagues are commonplace. Only recently have cases of sexual harassment started surfacing in so-called civilized societies, showing the extent of abuse of women in the workplace and schools. This is why Islām places such importance on the protection of a woman's chastity and honor.

# Getting Married

Islām requires both boys and girls to be chaste, pure and respectable. When a boy or girl reaches maturity, the next natural step is to seek a life companion and begin a family.  Muslims are encouraged to get married as soon as they are mature enough and have the means to do so.

When a boy or girl wishes to get married, his/her family should help him/her find a suitable husband or wife, who will make him/her happy.

They should look for a boy or a girl who is of good character and a practicing Muslim. When two people decide they want to get married, they should make their intentions public to avoid any misunderstandings. It is also advisable not to postpone the date of the marriage unnecessarily.

A Muslim girl should be treated with respect and honor. She is not to be treated as an object to be looked at. A Muslim girl takes pride in her chastity and honor, and a Muslim boy respects and admires a girl who is chaste and virtuous. Similarly, a Muslim girl admires a boy who is honorable and chaste and will be able to take on the responsibility of a family.
The Qur'ān describes the marital relationship as thus:

$$\text{هُنَّ لِبَاسٌ لَّكُمْ وَأَنتُمْ لِبَاسٌ لَّهُنَّ}$$

*The (women) are your garments and you (men) are their garment.*
*(Al-Baqarah 2:187)*

And as the garment comforts the body, protects it from the elements, beautifies it and hides its shame, so must a married couple do for each other. Islām requires that after marriage, a couple should be faithful to each other. In fact, one of the worst sins by Islāmic standards is *Zina,* or adultery.

## WE HAVE LEARNED:

* To protect his/her honor, a Muslim should behave modestly and avoid friendships with the opposite sex.
* Boys and girls should not be alone with each other.
* Muslims are encouraged to get married as soon as possible.

## EXERCISES

1. Why should Muslims avoid friendships with the opposite sex?
2. Is dating allowed in Islām? Discuss why or why not.

3.    If in mixed company, how should a boy behave?  How should a girl behave?

4.    Why do you think Allāh  has put certain restrictions on the way women present themselves before men?  Do men have as much responsibility to protect their chastity as women do?

5.    If Muslims don't date, how do they get married?  What qualities do they look for in a prospective mate?

6.    What is the wisdom in making your intentions for marriage public?

# LESSON 37

## THE ISLĀMIC WORK ETHIC

### The Need for Work

At the end of his education, every student hopes to find a good job, so he can settle down and provide his family with the necessities of life: food, clothing, and shelter. He hopes that his education will help him decide what career to choose and prepare him for success in his field of choice.

People need to work. Whether they work at home, as mothers and home-makers, or at a place of business, as professionals, people need the sense of accomplishment that they get from a hard day's work. Working helps a person develop moral strength and responsibility. In this regard, Rasūlullāh 🕮 said:

> *Nobody has ever eaten a better meal than that which*
> *one has earned by working with one's own hands.*
> (Transmitted by Bukhari)

### The Value of Work to the Community

In addition to individual development and providing livelihood, work has other values. Work is essential for active community development.

Many occupations are geared toward meeting the needs of the community. For example, farming, cooking, building, carpentry, weaving, dress-making provide food, shelter and clothing. Business trading brings products from one place to another into the hands of the people who need them.

Other occupations focus on creating a basis for the future through education and religious development. For example, teachers, *Imāms,* school principals, and mothers, as home educators, provide children the necessary tools for learning, so they may become responsible citizens in the future.

Occupations such as medicine, nursing, pharmacy and other health care fields are responsible for relieving the suffering of individuals and promoting the general health and welfare of the community.

Occupations in law and the armed services, such as judges, the police, prison service, and firemen serve to maintain order, protecting life and property to make the community safe.

Occupations such as collection of revenues and taxes and provision of services such as roads, electricity, water, education, health services are responsible for administration of the government.

There are too many types of work to list completely here, but we get an idea of the many occupations there are to choose from. From all these fields, a Muslim can choose a job that interests him and benefits other people as well.

## Value of Work as Worship

Work has another important value. When a job is done honestly with the intention to please Allāh ﷻ, it becomes a form of worship.

Allāh ﷻ says in the Qur'ān:

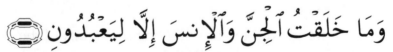

*I have only created Jinns and men that they may serve Me.*
(*Al-Dhariyat* 51:56)

If we work with the intention to serve Allāh ﷻ, our work becomes a service to Allāh ﷻ, which Allāh ﷻ will reward. Rasūlullāh ﷺ is reported to have said:

*Whoever works to earn an honest living (Halāl) acted on my Sunnah*
*and did not harm people will be admitted to Jannah (paradise)*
(Transmitted by Tirmidhi)

## Avoiding Unlawful Occupations

Of course, a Muslim cannot expect any reward from Allāh ﷻ if he chooses an occupation that is *Harām* (unlawful). Any occupation that requires duties that are un-Islāmic should be avoided, even if it offers good pay and excellent benefits. For example, if one sells beer and wine in his store, or becomes a worker in a casino, or an owner of a bar, he can only expect punishment and not reward from Allāh ﷻ. In addition, any occupation that requires sacrificing one's modesty, such as modeling swimsuits, is forbidden.

## Avoiding Unlawful Working Habits

If a person wants his work to be accepted as worship by Allāh ﷻ, he must work in a lawful and honest way. Cheating, stealing, bribery or corruption, laziness or refusal to work properly ruins the spiritual benefit of work.

Rasūlullāh ﷺ was noted as saying:

*On the Day of Judgment, Allāh will not speak to him*
*nor will he look at him, nor purify him for admission in*
*Jannah (paradise), who takes false oaths to increase his wealth.*
(Transmitted by Muslim)

If we want to serve Allāh ﷻ, we must offer good work, because Allāh ﷻ

will not accept corrupt offerings. Even if our dishonesty goes undetected by our employers, Allāh ﷻ will give us the due consequences of all our actions.

In addition to working honestly, we should also maintain good Islāmic manners at the workplace. Being polite and respectful with our co-workers and employers, never using indecent language, and being prompt with our work are all part of a Muslim's work ethic.

## WE HAVE LEARNED:

* Students should plan for their careers in the future.
* There are many honorable professions for a Muslim to choose from.
* A real Muslim should stay away from jobs that are *Harām*.

## EXERCISES

1.  What are the three main purposes and values of work?
2.  Name three types of work that are useful to the community.
3.  How can work become a service to Allāh ﷻ?
4.  Name two types of work that are *Harām* (unlawful).
5.  What sort of dishonest behavior must a Muslim avoid in his working habits?
6.  What did Rasūlullāh ﷺ say about honest work?
7.  Describe two common cases of dishonesty in present society. How could you avoid dishonest behavior in both cases?

# LESSON 38

## VOLUNTARY SERVICE TO ISLĀM AND THE COMMUNITY

### The Need to Help Islām and the Community

As we know, a Muslim has a duty to his parents, his family and to those in need. It is also beneficial for a Muslim to use his spare time to help the cause of Islām and the community.

### Cooperation

A Muslim can serve Allāh ﷻ and the community through individual efforts. However, he is likely to be more useful if he combines his efforts with the efforts of others who share his desire to help. By encouraging and supporting each other, they can achieve their goals more efficiently in a timely manner.

### How Can Young People Contribute to this Cause?

If there is an Islāmic organization in the area, young people can join it and form a youth wing. Through this organization, they can help with many useful services such as:

1. Organizing classes or lectures to improve their knowledge of Islām and the Arabic language of the Qur'ān.
2. Helping to build a *Masjid* or making improvements on the

local *Masjid*.

3. Helping with clean-up campaigns to keep the city clean.
4. Helping to raise money for any useful cause that will benefit the community.
5. Organizing workers for any cause that will benefit the community or an individual who is in need.
6. Working on *Dawah* by providing information on Islām for non-Muslims.

These are just a few examples of how you can contribute to Islām and your community. When you are older, you may find other ways to help.


## Supporting What is Right and Forbidding What is Wrong

Another way of helping your community is by using your knowledge of right and wrong, according to Islām:

كُنتُمْ خَيْرَ أُمَّةٍ أُخْرِجَتْ لِلنَّاسِ تَأْمُرُونَ بِالْمَعْرُوفِ وَتَنْهَوْنَ عَنِ الْمُنكَرِ وَتُؤْمِنُونَ بِاللَّهِ

*You are the best of Peoples evolved for humankind. Enjoining what is right, forbidding what is wrong, and believing in Allāh.....*
(*Āli 'Imrān* 3:110)

Every Muslim is expected to stand up for right and fight wrongdoing within the limits of his power. A *Hadīth* explains this expectation as follows:

*If you see something evil you should correct it with your hand,*
*and if that is not possible, correct it with your tongue,*
*and if that is not possible, you should hate it in your heart -*
*and that is the weakest (form) of faith.*
(Transmitted by Muslim)

So, if you see some evil being done and you have the power to stop it, you should do so. You should not ignore the evil. If however, you have no power to stop the evil directly, you should speak against it, either by warning the evil-doer or by calling on others to help stop the evil. If, due to weakness or oppression, you have no power even to speak against the evil, you should at least hate it in your heart and have the wish to change it. That is the weakest degree of faith. In any case, you should never accept the evil with peace of mind.

## WE HAVE LEARNED:

* We should donate some of our time to good causes.
* Working as a group helps to make our tasks easier.
* A Muslim should always stand up for good and oppose evil.

## EXERCISES

1. How can a young Muslim join others to help serve Islām and his or her community? Give two examples.
2. Explain what you should do to correct evil-doing, in accordance with the *Hadīth* of Rasūlullāh ﷺ.

# LESSON 39

## CONCLUSION TO PART I: THE PURPOSE OF ISLĀMIC TAHDHĪB AND AKHLĀQ

*Tahdhīb* and *Akhlāq* define the Islāmic way to serve Allāh ﷻ and be a useful member of society. As Muslims, our first and foremost purpose in life is to obey Allāh ﷻ. We need to obey Him, because He is our Creator. He controls our past, present, and future. Only He can give us what we need in this life and in the Hereafter. Allāh ﷻ loves us and has sent his guidance through His messengers. Through them, He sent His books, containing Divine instructions on how to lead a moral Islāmic life leading to success in the Hereafter.

He sent His Final Revelation, the Qur'ān, as His Book of guidance for all times to come. The Qur'ān is the best guide to Islāmic *Tahdhīb* and *Akhlāq*, clearly specifying the fundamental principles of Islāmic belief and practice. A believer knows that everything the Qur'ān has deemed *Halāl* is permissible, and whatever it has declared *Harām* is forbidden. The *Shariah* gives us the complete code of Islāmic Law.

Allāh ﷻ sent His last messenger, Muhammad ﷺ, as the ultimate model of Islāmic *Tahdhīb* and *Akhlāq*. Rasūlullāh ﷺ showed us how to practice the teachings of the Qur'ān. Umm al-Mu'minin, 'A'ishah ﵂, said about the Prophet ﷺ:

> "His *Akhlāq* (Morals) was the Qur'ān."

Therefore, as true Muslims we must believe and practice both the teachings of the Qur'ān and the *Sunnah* of Rasūlullāh ﷺ. The Qur'ān teaches us that obedience to the Messenger ﷺ is in fact the obedience to Allāh ﷻ:

$$\text{مَّن يُطِعِ ٱلرَّسُولَ فَقَدْ أَطَاعَ ٱللَّهَ}$$

*Whoever obeys the Messenger, indeed obeys Allāh.*
(*An-Nisa'* 4:80)

We learned earlier that Allāh ﷻ gave us the capacity to reason right from wrong. With the Qur'ān as a source of guidance, and Rasūlullāh ﷺ as the best example of how to live a pure and meaningful life, Muslims have all the necessities to find their way to the ultimate goal: success in the Hereafter, eternal bliss.

## Setting a Good Example

Allāh ﷻ wants Muslims not only to practice what they believe, but also spread these truths to others. A practicing Muslim is an excellent example to others - both Muslims and non-Muslims. By guiding other people to good conduct, he gains additional reward from Allāh ﷻ. If a Muslim exhibits good behavior, people will like and admire him and wish to follow his good example.

An obedient Muslim focuses on pleasing Allāh ﷻ, so he does not show off to impress others. Because he seeks only the reward that Allāh ﷻ can give him, he does not feel jealous or envious of others. He knows His Creator is witnessing his every action, so he is careful to be honest, decent, and kind to others. In seeking Allāh ﷻ's pleasure, he develops qualities that win him the respect and love of his fellow human beings.

## The Best Community

A Muslim individual is part of the *'Ummah,* the community of Islām. The Muslim *'Ummah* is the best community, because it was chosen to fulfill

149

Allāh ﷻ's mission. Allāh ﷻ also enjoins us to live up to His expectation:

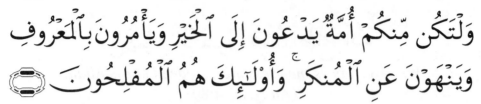

*Let there arise from amongst you a community inviting*
*to all that is good enjoining what is right, and forbidding*
*what is wrong: they are the one who are successful.*
(Āli 'Imran 3: 104)

Therefore, it is the duty of every Muslim, individually and collectively, to complete the mission of Islām by striving to set the best example for humanity and inviting other people to the righteous path of Islām.

Allāh ﷻ guides each of us to the right path. May Allāh ﷻ help us to be obedient to Him. May Allāh ﷻ help us to study and follow the Qur'ān and the *Sunnah* of His last Prophet ﷺ. May Allāh ﷻ help us to be excellent examples for humanity.

## The Best Examples Of Islāmic *Tahdhīb* and *Akhlāq*

Islāmic *Tahdhīb* and *Akhlāq* is not just a set of theories or a code of conduct. Through the lives of the prophets, *Sahābah,* and other pious Muslims, we see the practicality of *Tahdhīb* and *Akhlāq*. In the second part of the book, we will examine the lives and missions of the prophets of Allāh ﷻ, as described in the Qur'ān. We will also discuss the Sirah of our Prophet Muhammad, Rasūlullāh ﷺ, as related in the Qur'ān and the books of Ahadīth and *Sīrah*. All the prophets were the true models of Islāmic *Tahdhīb* and *Akhlāq*, but in the Prophet Muhammad ﷺ, we have the most perfect example.

The *Sahābah* of Rasūlullāh ﷺ came next to him as being the best models of Islāmic *Tahdhīb* and *Akhlāq*. Throughout history, the *'Ummah* of Islām has also produced the most beautiful characters of Islāmic faith. We should study the lives of all of them and follow their examples. In the second part of this book, we have given brief biographies of some *Ṣahābah* and other prominent Muslims as well. However, we encourage you to further your study of these and other biographies in other books that cover this subject in greater detail.

## WE HAVE LEARNED:

* Every good Muslim must obey Allāh ﷻ and His Rasūlullāh ﷺ .
* There are great rewards in this life and the next for those who obey Allāh's Commands.
* A Muslim must try his best in everything he does.

## EXERCISES

1. According to what we have learned, what is the main pur pose of the  *Tahdhīb*?
   (a) For our general knowledge,
   (b) For passing examinations,
   (c) For us to practice in daily life.
2. A Muslim who obeys Allāh ﷻ will be rewarded.
   Will the reward be found:
   (a) In this world?
   (b) In the Hereafter?
   (c) In both this world and the Hereafter?
3. How can a person find true peace of mind and happiness in this life?
4. What is the benefit of setting a good example as a Muslim?
5. Allāh ﷻ says in the Qur'ān that the Muslims form the best community for mankind because of a special mission. What is this mission?

# ISLAMIC *TAHDHĪB* AND *AKHLĀQ*

## Part II: Practice

# INTRODUCTORY NOTES ON SĪRAH
# FOR TEACHERS

Teaching *Sīrah* serves two important purposes. First, by learning about the life and times of the prophets and famous Muslims, students gain insight into the struggles through which Islām was born and has survived. Second, students can learn important moral lessons from the examples of these historical heroes of Islām.

It is to be noted that the Qur'an does not give full details in the biographies of the prophets. Further elaboration is to be found in the Jewish and Christian scriptures. However, in view of the way in which the Bible was written and compiled, it cannot be completely relied upon by Muslims as an accurate historical record. For this reason, the Qur'an gives corrections to the Biblical accounts in certain cases. When reading the Biblical versions of these stories, one must use the Qur'an and *Sunnah* as the defining criteria.

# LESSON 1

## AN INTRODUCTION TO THE MESSENGERS OF ALLĀH ﷻ

### Who Were the Prophets and Messengers of Allāh?

The prophets, or *Anbiyā*, were special men chosen and guided by Allāh ﷻ to bring His Message to mankind. There were many prophets chosen at different times among the nations of the world. Some were given Allāh's Divine Scriptures. These messengers are known as *Rusul*.

### What was Allāh's Message to the Prophets and Messengers ?

Allāh ﷻ revealed the Divine truths necessary to guide humanity to these chosen servants. The first of these truths is that God alone is the Creator of the heaven and the earth. The second truth is that after death, all men would be called to account for their deeds on earth. He gave them the good news that the true servants of Allāh ﷻ would be rewarded with joy and beauty in the Hereafter. He also warned that the pain of Hell awaited those who refused Allāh ﷻ's guidance and did evil deeds. Finally, He gave them guidelines for good conduct and how to live a good life in obedience to Him.

The duty of the Nabi or *Rusul* was to teach Allāh ﷻ's message to his people. Their job was not to force people to believe, because enlightenment would come only from Allāh ﷻ to those who earned and deserved it. They could only guide people towards enlightenment.

## What Kind of People Were the Prophets and Messengers?

Allāh ﷻ chose only good, truthful men as His prophets and messengers, so that people would trust them and learn how to live righteously from their example. The prophets and messengers of Allāh ﷻ were all very honest and faithful people.

## Who Were the Messengers of Allāh?

Twentyfive of the messengers are named in the Qur'ān, as follows:

> Ādam, Nūh, Ibrahīm, Lūt, Isma'il, Ishāq, Ya'qūb, Yūsuf, Ṣālih, Shu'aib, Hud, Yūnus, Mūsa, Hārūn, Ayyūb, Dawūd, Sulaimān, Ilyās, Al-Yasa', Dhul-kifl, Idris, Zakariyyā, Yahyā, 'Isa, and Muhammad (peace and blessings of Allāh be upon them all).

## What was the Religion Taught by the Messengers of Allāh ﷻ?

The messengers of Allāh ﷻ all believed in Allāh ﷻ and submitted their hearts and minds to Him. One who submits to Allāh ﷻ is a Muslim. By this definition, all the messengers of Allāh ﷻ were Muslims.

However, it was through Prophet Muhammad ﷺ, the last prophet and messenger, that the religion of all the messengers and prophets was given its full and final form and its name-Islām.

All the messengers taught their people to submit to Allāh ﷾ and some of them did. But after the death of these messengers , some of their later followers modified the original teachings by adding their own ideas. Slowly, their beliefs began to shift away from submission to Allāh ﷾. Eventually, these beliefs gave rise to different religions.

Islām, which means "submission to Allāh ﷾," is the only true religion, the religion of the prophets. The Qur'ān, upon which Islām is based, is the only Holy Book that has never been altered and that has remained in its original form.

Rasulullah ﷺ said:

> *Every child is born in the natural religion of Allāh* ﷾
> *(i.e. Islām); it is his parents that bring him up as*
> *a Christian, or a Jew, or a Magian (another religion).*
> (Transmitted by Bukhāri)

This means that Islām is the natural religion for humanity. It is clear and easy to understand, and thereby, it meets the challenges of human logic and reason.

### Are There Any Prophets in the World Today?

Allāh ﷾ sent the Prophet Muhammad ﷺ as the last of the prophets. In the Qur'ān, he is called the *"Khātim an-Nabiyyīn"* (the Seal of the Prophets).

Allāh ﷻ also says in the Qur'ān:

ٱلْيَوْمَ أَكْمَلْتُ لَكُمْ دِينَكُمْ وَأَتْمَمْتُ عَلَيْكُمْ
نِعْمَتِى وَرَضِيتُ لَكُمُ ٱلْإِسْلَـٰمَ دِينًا ۚ

*...This day have I perfected your religion for you, completed my favor upon you, and have chosen for you Islām as your religion.*
(*Al-Ma'idah* 5: 3)

Rasulullah ﷺ required his *Ṣahābah* رضي الله عنهم (companions) to memorize the Qur'ān and write it down in his presence to prevent error or distortion. It has never been changed.

The Qur'ān is the true and final message of Allāh ﷻ. Since it has never been changed or lost, there is no need for any new messenger to bring a revised message. Within it, we find the answer to all of lifeís questions.

WE HAVE LEARNED:

* Allāh ﷻ has guided mankind through messengers and prophets.
* Messengers and prophets are the highest examples of goodness.
* Rasūlullāh ﷺ is the last and final Messenger and Prophet, none shall come after him, ever.

# LESSON 2

---

## LIVES OF THE EARLY PROPHETS

### Sources

All of our knowledge about the earlier prophets comes from the Qur'ān. Prophet Muhammad ﷺ also gave further information about some of them in the *Ḥadīth*. In most cases, the Qur'ān does not usually tell the whole story of each prophet. It only tells the most important things, in such a way that we can learn many lessons from them.

Here, we shall retell some of what the Qur'ān says about the prophets. When students are older, they will, *Insha' Allāh*, read the stories in the Qur'ān themselves.

# Prophet Ādam

We have already learned about how Ādam was created by Allāh ﷻ and what happened when *Shaiṭan* refused to bow to him (see Book 1, *Tawḥīd* and *Fiqh*, Lesson 15).

Allāh ﷻ then created a woman named Haww'a to be Ādam's companion. Allāh ﷻ placed both of them in a garden in Paradise, a pleasant place to live. He told them they were free to eat the fruits in the garden, but He warned them not to eat the fruit of one particular tree or they would become wrongdoers. Prophet Ādam ﷺ and Hawwa', followed Allāh's directions and enjoyed every fruit of the garden, remembering not to go near that forbidden tree.

But *Shaiṭan* whispered into their hearts that the fruit of that tree was very delicious. He lied to them, saying that the fruit would make them like angels, and they would live forever. Prophet Ādam ﷺ and Haww'a forgot Allāh's warning and ate the fruit. As soon as they had eaten it, they felt ashamed and knew that they had done something wrong.

They were sorry for being weak and disobedient, and they both prayed to Allāh ﷻ to forgive them. Allāh ﷻ did forgive them both, but He ordered that they live on the earth for some time. He also told them that they would be allowed to return to Paradise only if they and their children obeyed His Commandments and followed His Messages.

Allāh ﷻ made Ādam ﷺ a prophet, so that he could show his family how to obey Allāh ﷻ. Prophet Ādam ﷺ taught his people, and after his death, Allāh ﷻ chose other prophets, as He had promised, from among Prophet Ādam's children and grandchildren.

# Prophet Nūh ﷺ

Long after the time of Ādam ﷺ , there lived another prophet named Nūh ﷺ . Allāh ﷻ sent him to lead his people who had become disobedient. They did not worship Allāh ﷻ and were unkind and cruel.

Prophet Nūh ﷺ tried for a long time to teach them the truth about Allāh ﷻ, but they refused to listen. The wise prophet warned them that if they continued to disobey Allāh ﷻ, they would earn His punishment. This only made the disbelievers laugh at Nūh ﷺ .

After many years of struggle, Prophet Nūh ﷺ prayed to Allāh ﷻ for help in defeating these people who were spreading evil on the earth. Allāh ﷻ heard his prayers and told Prophet Nūh ﷺ to build a ship. The people were very surprised when they saw Prophet Nūh ﷺ building a large ship, since their land was not near any sea or lake. They laughed at him even more and said he had become insane.

When the ship was completed, it began to rain. Allāh ﷻ told Prophet Nūh ﷺ to board the ship with all of the people who had faith in Allāh ﷻ, one pair, a male and a female, of every animal, and some food.

The rain kept falling. Dark clouds and storms covered the sky, and the rivers burst their banks. Water filled the valleys, and it seemed that water was coming out of the ground.

Prophet Nūh ﷺ called to one of his sons, who had not heeded Allāh's Message, to join him on the ship, so that he would not be left among the disbelievers. But his son rejected the warning, certain that he would escape the floods by going up a high hill where the water could not reach him.

Prophet Nūh ﷺ tried to warn him that the only way he could be protected was to accept the Message of Allāh ﷻ. But Nūh's son ignored his warning, and a great wave came and swept him away along with the other disbelievers.

And so, Prophet Nūh ﷺ and the people and animals in the ship were saved from the flood. The water rose so high that the whole area, including the hills and mountains, was under water. At last, the rain stopped, the water went down and the ship came to rest on the land. Prophet Nūh ﷺ and those who were with him came out from the ship and thanked Allāh ﷻ for saving them. Under Prophet Nūh's guidance, the remaining people followed the right path of life, as directed by Allāh ﷻ.

# Prophet Hūd ﷺ

The people of 'Ād are believed to have lived in Southeastern Arabia. They were a very powerful tribe. They built fine houses and towers on the hills. Since they were hard working, they had plenty to eat from the land. Yet, they did not worship Allāh ﷻ or thank Him for the comfort and happiness of their lives.

Allāh ﷻ chose Hūd ﷺ as His prophet to the people of 'Ād. Prophet Hūd ﷺ called on his people to worship Allāh ﷻ alone and to thank Him, since all that they were enjoying was from Him. He warned them that if they did not change their ungrateful ways, Allāh ﷻ would punish them.

But the people said: "You are either mad or you are a liar. We do not believe that Allāh sent you, and we will not abandon our gods. Nothing can happen to us. Let your Allāh's punishment come. We don't believe you."

Hūd ﷺ said: "I am not a liar. Indeed, I am sent to you as a prophet of Allāh. Is it not Allāh who has given you wealth and your beautiful houses? Do you think your houses will last forever? If you do not repent, Allāh will destroy you and give wealth and power to other people."

Still, the people of 'Ād did not leave their false gods. Prophet Hūd ﷺ felt unhappy that he could not save them, but he and the others who believed him left the people of 'Ād to escape from the punishment that was about to befall them.

Soon, the people saw a cloud coming toward them. At first, they thought it was filled with rain. Instead, the cloud brought a terrible wind that destroyed them with all their gardens, lands and houses, and left 'Ād like a desert, with tracks of sand blowing across the place they had once been so proud of.

# Prophet Sālih ﷺ

Prophet Ṣālih ﷺ lived among the people of Thamūd, who are believed to have lived in Northern Arabia, near the border of Syria. They built palaces and lived in houses cut in the rocks and mountains with beautiful gardens full of fruit trees and springs of cool water.

Prophet Ṣālih ﷺ appealed to his people to leave their false gods and worship only Allāh ﷻ. He tried to make them understand that he was Allāh's prophet, sent to guide them on the right path. He told them that if they turned to Allāh ﷻ, He would forgive them.

Some of the people believed him, but most of the rich and important people laughed at him. They said: "We look at you as a man like us. Show us a sign, if you can, so we can see that you are telling the truth." The sign they asked for was a she-camel to appear out of the mountains, who would give birth to a baby camel upon her arrival.

So Prophet Ṣālih ﷺ prayed to Allāh ﷻ, and He sent the sign they asked for. Prophet Ṣālih ﷺ warned his people: "This camel is a sign for you from Allāh. Let her eat the grass of Allāh's earth and drink from our springs. Do not harm her. If you do hurt her, a terrible punishment will fall on you."

But the people of Thamūd were very disobedient. They stopped the camel from drinking the water and killed

Then they said to Prophet Ṣālih ﷺ : "Now bring Allāh's punishment which you told us would come."

They refused to believe the prophet and disobeyed Allāh's Command. Indeed, the due punishment followed. Ṣāliḥ  left them, and after three days, a terrible earthquake destroyed them along with all their houses and gardens, and their power and wealth were gone forever.

# Prophet Ibrāhīm ﷺ

Prophet Ibrāhīm ﷺ was born in Mesopotamia, a land now called Iraq. The people of that time had forgotten to worship One God. They worshipped the sun, the moon and the stars. In their places of worship there were idols made of clay and stone.

As a young man, Ibrāhīm ﷺ was always deep in thought. One night, he looked at a bright star and said: "That is my Lord!" But when the star disappeared soon after dawn, he knew that it was not God. Another time, he looked at the moon and said: "That is my Lord!" But when the moon also disappeared in the morning, he knew that it was not God. At last, he watched the sunrise and said: "This is the greatest of them-this is my Lord." But when the sun disappeared at the end of the day, he knew that God was neither the stars nor the moon nor the sun. He realized that God is unseen and is the Creator of all of them.

Prophet Ibrāhīm ﷺ told his people: "My people, I am free of your guilt of worshipping other gods besides Allāh. I firmly and truly turn my face to Him who created the heaven and the earth, and I shall never worship any god but Allāh."

Allāh ﷻ chose Ibrāhīm ﷺ as His prophet, and guided him throughout his life. Prophet Ibrāhīm ﷺ began to preach to his people against worshipping many gods. This made the people angry, especially the priests who served the idols.

To show people how useless their idols were, Prophet Ibrāhīm ﷺ came up with a plan. One night, when all the people were away, he went to the temple (the house of the idols) and broke all of the idols, except the biggest one. He left that one alone for a reason. When the priests and people returned, they were shocked and asked: "Who has done this to our gods?" They remembered that Prophet Ibrāhīm ﷺ had spoken against their idols, so they called him and asked him whether he had broken the idols.

Prophet Ibrāhīm ﷺ replied: "Perhaps the biggest idol did it. Why don't you ask your gods?"

They said in anger: "You know our gods do not speak!"

Prophet Ibrāhīm ﷺ replied: "Do you worship things that cannot help you or harm you?"

The people felt foolish that their gods could not even save themselves or even tell who had attacked them, and in their anger, they tried to kill Ibrāhīm ﷺ by throwing him into a fire.

But it was not Allāh's Will that Ibrāhīm ﷺ should be killed, so He cooled the fire to protect Prophet Ibrāhīm ﷺ from harm. The king heard of what Prophet Ibrāhīm ﷺ was preaching and sent for him. In front of all his important subjects, he questioned Prophet Ibrāhīm ﷺ: "Who is the invisible god you are preaching about?"

Unafraid, Prophet Ibrāhīm ﷺ answered: "My God is the One who gives and takes away life."

The king answered arrogantly: "I can do that," declaring that he could kill or spare the lives of his people as he wished.

Prophet Ibrāhīm ﷺ then asked the king: "My God is the One Who causes the sun to rise in the east. Can you make the sun rise in the west?" The king could make no such assertion.

Prophet Ibrāhīm ﷺ had a few followers who also believed in Allāh ﷻ but most of the people and the priests hated him and his message. Even Prophet Ibrāhīm ﷺ's father, Azar, did not believe Ibrāhīm's message and was angry with him because of all the trouble he had caused. Prophet Ibrāhīm ﷺ tried his best to change his father's mind, but failed, and his father told him to go away.

So Prophet Ibrāhīm ﷺ, his wife, Sarah , and some relatives and followers left Mesopotamia and traveled far away across mountains and deserts to the Land of Canaan. Once there, they were free to worship Allāh ﷻ in the way Allāh ﷻ taught Ibrāhīm ﷺ. Prophet Ibrāhīm ﷺ's only sadness was that he had no child who could take over his mission and his leadership when he died, so he used to pray to Allāh ﷻ for children.

When Prophet Ibrāhīm ﷺ was an old man his second wife, Hājar, gave birth to a son, Isma'il ﷺ. Prophet Ibrāhīm ﷺ was very happy. After some time, his first wife, Sarah, also gave birth to a son, Ishāq ﷺ. Both of these sons became prophets when they grew up. Prophet Ibrāhīm ﷺ became the forefather of the Arabs through his elder son, Isma'il ﷺ , and the forefather of the Jews through his younger son, Ishāq ﷺ .

Sarah , Ishāq ﷺ and Prophet Ibrāhīm's followers stayed in Canaan, but Ibrāhīm ﷺ led Hajar and the baby Isma'il ﷺ to the Valley of Makkah, and settled them there to make their new home. It was a place of stony hills with no water. The baby Isma'il ﷺ began to cry for water, so his mother put him on the ground and went to look for water. She climbed the little hill of Safa and ran to another hill, called Marwah, to search for water but none was to be found. She ran back and forth in desperation, praying to Allāh ﷻ for help. When she returned to her child, she found a spring of water flowing out from the ground at Isma'il's feet. The spring water is called *Zam Zam,* and its water continues to flow. It can be obtained from taps near the Ka'bah.

After some years, Prophet Ibrāhīm ﷺ had a dream that made him very sad. He saw in his dream that Allāh ﷻ commanded him to sacrifice his son Isma'il ﷺ ! When a prophet had a dream of this kind, he knew he had to obey, because it was guidance from Allāh ﷻ. He was very sad, because he had waited so long for a son and he loved Isma'il ﷺ very much. But he knew that to obey Allāh's Command is more important than all that we love in this world.

Prophet Ibrāhīm ﷺ told Isma'il ﷺ about his dream. Isma'il ﷺ told his father that he was ready to die according to Allāh's Command.

Prophet Ibrāhīm ﷺ took Isma'il ﷺ outside the town and prepared to sacrifice his son. But as he raised the knife, Allāh ﷻ commanded him to stop: "Ibrāhīm, you have already fulfilled the vision."

Allāh ﷻ accepted Prophet Ibrāhīm ﷺ's perfect obedience and ordered him to sacrifice a ram in place of his son.

So, Prophet Ibrāhīm ﷺ slaughtered the ram as the sign of his complete obedience to Allāh ﷻ. To this day, Muslims all over the world slaughter a ram or other animal on the *'Id al-Adha* (feast of sacrifice). The sacrifice of a ram is a sign of our own obedience and submission to Allāh ﷻ and a reminder of the example of Prophet Ibrāhīm ﷺ.

Allāh ﷻ then commanded Prophet Ibrāhīm ﷺ and Isma'il ﷺ to build the *Ka'bah* as a house of worship for the One God. They did so, and Allāh ﷻ blessed the *Ka'bah* and the town of Makkah. From that time onwards, people have traveled from far and near to worship Allāh ﷻ at the *Ka'bah*.

However, after the time of Prophet Ibrāhīm ﷺ and Isma'īl ﷺ , some people brought idols to the *Ka'bah* and made it a house of idolworship. Several thousand years later, it was Prophet Muhammad ﷺ , (an Arab descended from Prophets Ibrāhīm ﷺ and Isma'īl ﷺ), who at last cleared away all the idols from the *Ka'bah* and brought the people back to the worship of One God.

When a Muslim goes to Makkah for Hajj or *'Umrah,* he will find that many of the things he will do and see remind him of the great events in the life of Prophet Ibrāhīm ﷺ, Hajar and Isma'īl ﷺ .

Prophet Ibrāhīm ﷺ's story teaches us many lessons about courage, patience and obedience to Allāh ﷻ. Allāh ﷻ made Ibrāhīm ﷺ a great prophet, the father of great nations and the *Imam* (leader) of all nations. Millions of people, Muslims, Christians and Jews, worship the One God.

In the Qur'ān, Prophet Ibrāhīm ﷺ is called, "al-Khalil," which means "the Friend (of Allāh ﷻ)." This shows what an excellent man he was, and how dear he is to Allāh ﷻ.

Prophet Ibrāhīm ﷺ was also loved and respected by the Rasūlullāh ﷺ many centuries later. When someone addressed Prophet Muhammad ﷺ, "You are the best of creatures," he modestly refused this title, saying: "That was (Prophet) Ibrāhīm ﷺ."

Peace be upon Prophet Ibrāhīm ﷺ and on all the other prophets.

# Prophet Lūt ﷺ

Prophet Lūt ﷺ was a nephew of Prophet Ibrāhīm ﷺ. He left Mesopotamia with his uncle. When he reached Canaan he went to live in a town lying to the east. The people of this town were idolworshippers, and they had many evil customs. Prophet Lūt ﷺ begged them to believe in Allāh ﷻ and to leave their bad ways; but most of the people refused to listen to him and made his life very miserable.

After many years of turmoil, Allāh ﷻ sent three angels in the shape of men to Prophet Lūt ﷺ to tell him that Allāh ﷻ was going to destroy the town. They told Prophet Lūt ﷺ and his people to leave the town that night. The people of the town wanted to harm the angels and Prophet Lūt ﷺ, but Prophet Lūt ﷺ shut his doors against the crowd and waited until the night.

In the quiet of the night, Prophet Lūt ﷺ, his family and those who secretly believed in Allāh ﷻ left the town. Unfortunately, Prophet Lūt ﷺ's wife stayed behind. She refused to believe in Allāh's Message. At sunrise, when Prophet Lūt ﷺ and the others were safely away from the town, they heard a terrible noise as the city was destroyed by a great earthquake and falling stones.

The remains of that city may still be seen, covered by the desert sand. It serves as a reminder and a sign to those who do not take the Words of Allāh's prophets seriously.

# Prophet Shuʻaib ﷺ

Prophet Shuʻaib ﷺ was chosen as a prophet for the people of Madian. They are believed to have inhabited Northwest Arabia, between the Sinai Peninsula and the Dead Sea.

He called on them to worship only Allāh ﷻ and to behave fairly in their trading, since they used to cheat people in many different ways. He also warned them about their bad behavior toward those who believed and tried to do good.

But the people were proud and refused to accept his advice. They told Prophet Shuʻaib ﷺ and those who followed him that they would drive them out of the city if they refused to worship many gods.

Prophet Shuʻaib ﷺ and his followers prayed for Allāh ﷻ's help, and their prayer was answered. They were saved from the punishment that came, but an earthquake destroyed the people of Madian, and their houses and gardens became a desert.

# Prophet Yūsuf ﷺ

Prophet Ishāq ﷺ (the second son of Prophet Ibrāhīm ﷺ) had a son named Ya'qūb ﷺ, who was also a prophet. Prophet Ya'qūb ﷺ had twelve sons. One of them was named Yūsuf ﷺ and he was a very good and a handsome boy. His father loved him very much.

Yūsuf ﷺ had eleven brothers ten older than him and one younger. The older brothers were jealous because of their father's special love for Yūsuf ﷺ.

Out of jealousy, the brothers planned to get rid of Yūsuf ﷺ. They led him to a place far away from their home and pushed him down a dry well. Then they put some sheep's blood on Yūsuf's clothes and took it to their father saying: "We left Yūsuf alone for a while, and a wolf ate him! Look, we found his clothes drenched with blood!"

The brothers pretended to be upset, but Prophet Ya'qūb ﷺ did not believe them, and he continued to believe that Yūsuf ﷺ was alive. He prayed to Allāh ﷻ to return Yūsuf ﷺ to him. He cried so much that he started losing his eyesight and became almost blind. He never again trusted his sons.

Meanwhile in the well, Prophet Yūsuf ﷺ also prayed to Allāh ﷻ to save him. Allāh ﷻ assured him that he would live to reveal his brothers' deception at a time when they would not recognize him. After a while, some travelers found Yūsuf ﷺ. They took him with them to Egypt and sold him as a slave.

A nobleman bought him, and he worked faithfully in his master's house. However, he had a problem: his master's wife fell in love with his handsome looks and good manners. She wanted him to love her in the same way, but Prophet Yūsuf ﷺ refused. One day, while her husband was out, she told Prophet Yūsuf ﷺ of her love for him. Prophet Yūsuf ﷺ tried to get away from her, but she grabbed onto his shirt and tore it as he tried to escape. At that moment, the master returned and saw them. The wife lied, saying it was Prophet Yūsuf ﷺ who had attacked her. Being an honest man, her husband realized that the incident was his wife's fault and believed Yūsuf ﷺ.

The women of the town laughed at the nobleman's behavior. After all, falling in love with a slave was unthinkable. So, the wife invited these women to a dinner party at her house to show them Prophet Yūsuf ﷺ. When they saw his great beauty, they were so surprised that their knives slipped from the fruit they were cutting, and they cut their hands. They declared that he was not a man, but a noble angel. The wife was pleased and said: "This, then, is the one about whom you have been blaming me." She threatened Prophet Yūsuf ﷺ that he would be imprisoned if he did not obey her. The women did not blame her again, since some of them had also fallen in love with Prophet Yūsuf ﷺ.

Prophet Yūsuf ﷺ said that he would rather go to prison than be led astray by the women. He took no interest in them and continued his modest and good behavior. The women became angry, and their husbands became annoyed because they could not tolerate their wives' obsession with a slave. As a result, Prophet Yūsuf ﷺ was unjustly sent to prison on false charges, even though everyone knew he was innocent.

He spent some years in prison, but he always had faith that Allāh ﷻ would help him out of his troubles. The other prisoners liked and trusted him. As a prophet, he could understand the meaning of dreams, and thereby, he was able to explain the prisoners' dreams to them.

The pharaoh of Egypt had been having a particular dream, over and over again, and he wanted someone to explain it to him. One of the pharaoh's servants, who had earlier been in prison with Prophet Yūsuf ﷺ, remembered that he could interpret dreams. The servant recommended Prophet Yūsuf ﷺ to the pharaoh.

The pharaoh sent the servant to ask Prophet Yūsuf ﷺ about the dream, and Yūsuf ﷺ explained: "the pharaoh's dream means that there will be good harvest for seven years. For the next seven years, there will be bad harvests, and the people will go hungry. Therefore, he should save grain during the good years for use in the bad years."

The pharaoh sent for Prophet Yūsuf ﷺ and talked to him. He liked his manner and his noble appearance. Prophet Yūsuf ﷺ told him that he had been put in prison for something that was not his fault. The pharaoh sent for the women, and at last, they told the truth, clearing Prophet Yūsuf ﷺ of any wrongdoing.

The pharaoh liked and admired Prophet Yūsuf's personality so much that he made him the controller of the food stores for the entire country. What a sudden change in Prophet Yūsuf's fortune--from prisoner to top official!

The seven good harvests came just as Prophet Yūsuf ﷺ had foretold. The seven bad harvests followed, but the people began to use the grain that had been stored.

The same famine and hunger was felt in Canaan, the land where Prophet Yūsuf's father and brothers were still living. Ten of the brothers traveled to Egypt to buy grain from the stores that were under Yūsuf's control. They did not recognize Prophet Yūsuf ﷺ, who was now a grown man dressed in fine Egyptian clothes. Prophet Yūsuf ﷺ knew them, but he did not tell them who he was. He only told them to bring their younger brother, Benjamin, the next time they came or he would give them no more grain.

The brothers told their father about this, and Ya'qūb ﷺ was afraid to let his other son go with them. But when they opened the sacks of grain, they found that Prophet Yūsuf ﷺ had put their own merchandise, which they had offered Yūsuf ﷺ as payment for the grain, inside the sacks. They were all grateful for his kindness.

Ya'qūb ﷺ allowed the brothers to go back to Egypt with Benjamin. Prophet Yūsuf ﷺ secretly told Benjamin who he was, and his younger brother was very happy.

Before the brothers' departure, Prophet Yūsuf ﷺ hid the Pharaoh's drinking cup in a sack of grain on his youngest brother's camel.

When the guards searched the travelers, the cup was found in Benjamin's sack. Benjamin was detained, while the others went home with the grain. When Ya'qūb ﷺ heard what had happened, he felt sad, but he still hoped and prayed that he might see his two beloved sons again.

The brothers again journeyed to Egypt, very poor and desperate for grain. This time, Prophet Yūsuf ﷺ revealed to them who he was. The brothers felt very ashamed. They had wanted to kill him, but in return, Yūsuf ﷺ had treated them well. They begged Prophet Yūsuf ﷺ to forgive them, so Prophet Yūsuf ﷺ asked Allāh ﷻ to forgive them all. Prophet Yūsuf ﷺ gave them his shirt to take to his father.

As the brothers drew near their father's place, Prophet Ya'qūb ﷺ felt joyful and said he could even smell the sweet scent of his dear son, Yūsuf ﷺ. The brothers told their father the news. In his joy, he placed Prophet Yūsuf's shirt on his face, and miraculously, he was able to see again.

Prophet Ya'qūb ﷺ and the whole family went to Prophet Yūsuf ﷺ in Egypt, where they were very happy. Prophet Ya'qūb ﷺ and Prophet Yūsuf ﷺ had always behaved with patience and trusted Allāh ﷻ. So indeed, Allāh ﷻ rewarded their patience.

The family settled in Egypt and Prophet Yūsuf ﷺ preached the religion of Allāh ﷻ to the Egyptians for the rest of his life. With others, they formed a community of believers in Egypt that remained there in peace until the time of Prophet Mūsa , whose story follows.

The great lessons from the life of Prophet Yūsuf ﷺ are: (a) Never give up hope for Allāh ﷻ's help and mercy, even in the worst situation; (b) Obey Allāh ﷻ faithfully whatever other people may do to try to change your mind; (c) If someone hurts you, do not take revenge on him, even when you have the power to do so. Treat him well, and he may eventually see his fault, and feel sorry.

# Prophet Mūsa ﷺ

We learned about how Prophet Yūsuf ﷺ and his eleven brothers settled in Egypt. These brothers had many children, and their children had children, until after some time, their numbers were enormous. They all believed in the One God, as they had been taught by their Prophets Ibrāhīm ﷺ, Ishāq ﷺ, Ya'qūb ﷺ and Yūsuf ﷺ. These people became known as the Israelites.

The Egyptians were still worshipping many gods and goddesses. They hated the Israelites because the Israelites were regarded as foreigners in Egypt, and yet, they had increased in number and became powerful in Egypt.

The pharaoh of that time decided to stop the Israelites from holding high posts in Egypt. They were made to do hard labor, and were treated like slaves. But still their numbers grew and the pharaoh feared that they might rebel against him.

So the pharaoh gave an order that all Israelite baby boys should be killed. Many little boys were killed. Life became full of hardship, loss and sadness for the Israelites.

It was during this time that Prophet Mūsa ﷺ was born. His mother feared that he would be killed too. But Allāh ﷻ inspired her to put the baby in a box and float the box down the River Nile. The pharaoh's wife found the box on the riverbank. Mūsa's elder sister watched her. The pharaoh's wife took the baby from the box. She fell in love with the beautiful baby and decided to keep him.

The pharaoh's wife looked for a wetnurse to give milk to the baby.

Mūsa's sister saw her chance and told her she could bring a wet-nurse. So she ran and beckoned Mūsa's mother! Mūsa's mother was very happy. She thanked Allāh ﷻ that she was able to nurse her own lovely son.

Prophet Mūsa ﷺ grew up in the pharaoh's palace where he received a good education and the best of everything. But he knew he was an Israelite by birth and that he must worship One God. He felt sorry for his people who were unhappy in Egypt.

One day, Prophet Mūsa ﷺ a saw an Israelite fighting with an Egyptian. The Israelite called for his help, and Prophet Mūsa ﷺ a hit the Egyptian. He did not mean to kill him, but the man died. Prophet Mūsa ﷺ found himself in grave trouble.

Prophet Mūsa ﷺ a left Egypt and took refuge in the land of Midian. One day, out of kindness, he helped two young women water their flocks of sheep. Because of his kindness, the women's old father invited Prophet Mūsa ﷺ a to stay with him. Later, he gave Prophet Mūsa ﷺ a one of his daughters in marriage.

Some years after this, Prophet Mūsa ﷺ was traveling with his family, when he saw a fire in a valley. He left his family and went to look at the fire. When he came near it he heard a voice: "I am Allāh, your Lord. I have chosen you as a prophet for your people. Go to the pharaoh with your brother, Hārūn ﷺ. Speak to the pharaoh gently. Maybe, he will take your advice and fear God. Ask the pharaoh to let the Israelites leave Egypt in peace."

Allāh ﷻ gave Prophet Mūsa ﷺ two signs to prove to the pharaoh that he sent him. He told Prophet Mūsa ﷺ to throw his staff on the ground; it became a living snake. He told him to pick it up, and it turned back into a staff. Allāh ﷻ then told Prophet Mūsa ﷺ to put his hand on his chest, under his robe, and when he took it out, it was white and shining.

Prophet Mūsa ﷺ and Hārūn ﷺ were afraid of what the pharaoh would do when they preached to him, but Allāh ﷻ told them not to fear, as He would be with them.

They told the pharaoh that they were sent by Allāh ﷻ to preach to him. The pharaoh tried to trap them in argument, so that they would abuse the Egyptian gods and their worshippers. This would cause people to hate them and call for their death. But they avoided pharaoh's trap and spoke only for Allāh ﷻ, Who made the earth and all of its plants and animals, and allowed humans to enjoy His creation. They told the pharaoh that Allāh ﷻ would bring them to life after death and reward or punish them for their actions on earth.

Prophet Mūsa ﷺ a showed the pharaoh the signs Allāh ﷻ had given him. But when the pharaoh saw the staff turn into a snake, and the light of Prophet Mūsa ﷺ's hand, he accused Prophet Mūsa ﷺ of being a magician. He told him the magicians of Egypt could do the same or better, and he sent for them to come and compete with Prophet Mūsa ﷺ in magic.

On the day of a great festival, the magicians arrived and in front of the pharaoh and many other people they threw their staffs. Using their tricks, the sticks appeared to move like snakes. Prophet Mūsa ﷺ threw his staff, and when it became a snake, it swallowed up all the magic snakes of the magicians. The magicians knew at once that this was not a trick like their own. They said: "We believe in the God of Mūsa and Hārūn."

The pharaoh was very angry. They had failed to do what he wanted, and now, they dared to agree with his enemy, Prophet Mūsa ﷺ. He ordered his men to cut off the magicians' hands and feet to punish them, and to nail their bodies to palm trees until their death. The magicians replied that their faith in the God of all the worlds was complete. Let pharaoh punish them in this world; his power could not reach beyond death.

Then Allāh ﷻ sent punishments, one after the other, on the pharaoh and his people. The pharaoh would beg Prophet Mūsa ﷺ a to pray to his God to take away the punishment, and he would promise to let the Israelites go out of Egypt. But whenever the punishment ceased, he would change his mind, and break his promises.

When the pharaoh again promised to let them go, Allāh ﷻ told Prophet Mūsa ﷺ to prepare his people to leave at night.

In the morning, when the pharaoh heard that Prophet Mūsa ﷺ's followers had gone, he led his army after them. The Israelites reached the sea and saw the Egyptian army coming. They were afraid, but Allāh ﷻ guided Prophet Mūsa ﷺ to strike the sea with his staff. When he did, the water receded, leaving a dry path on which the Israelites crossed. The pharaoh and his army followed them along this dry path, but when the Israelites safely reached the other side of the sea, the waters closed in. The pharaoh and his great army were drowned and punished for cruelty and refusal to accept Allāh ﷻ's guidance.

Prophet Mūsa ﷺ and his people now entered the land of Sinai, whose people were idolworshippers, like the Egyptians. Some of the Israelites admired these idols, which they could see and touch.

Allāh ﷻ called Prophet Mūsa ﷺ to spend forty days on a mountain, where Allāh ﷻ revealed to him His commandments and laws for his people. They must worship only Him, the One True God. They must not kill a fellow man. They must not steal or do bad things to others.

While Prophet Mūsa ﷺ was away on the mountain, some of the Israelites did a very bad thing. They made a calf out of gold and worshipped it. When Prophet Mūsa ﷺ came down from the mountain, he was very angry and destroyed the golden calf. He warned his people against the evil of forgetting the One God who helped them out of slavery in Egypt and saved them from the pharaoh's army. The people felt ashamed. Prophet Mūsa ﷺ then taught them the commandments that Allāh ﷻ had revealed to him on the mountain, and they promised never to be unfaithful again. This revelation to Prophet Mūsa ﷺ is called the *Tawrāt*.

However, the Israelites gave Prophet Mūsa ﷺ trouble right up to his death. He wanted to move on to Canaan, but the Israelites were afraid of the pagan tribes who then lived in Canaan. The Israelites rebelled and refused to go on. Therefore, they had to stay in the desert area of Sinai for forty years before they entered Canaan. By that time, Prophet Mūsa ﷺ had died.

Prophet Mūsa ﷺ was a great prophet. He was an ordinary man whom Allāh ﷻ called to do extraordinary things. His whole life was a struggle; from the time he was born until his death. The greatest quality he had was a firm faith in Allāh ﷻ that gave him courage and endurance as a leader of men. He was also a patient person. He loved his people and showed great patience with them inspite of their continuous disobedience. He showed firmness in dealing with the disbelievers and kindness in correcting their weaknesses. He was disenchanted with them but never abandoned them.

# Prophet Yūnus ﷺ

The story of Prophet Yūnus ﷺ describes what happened to a prophet who lost patience. Yūnus ﷺ was sent to the people of a big town, believed to be Ninevah, the capital of Assyria.

Prophet Yūnus ﷺ preached to them to believe in Allāh ﷻ and to do good, but they refused to listen. Prophet Yūnus ﷺ became angry and left the town. He traveled in a ship across the sea "like a runaway slave." There was a great storm, and as a result of an incident, his fellow passengers threw him out of the ship. He fell in the sea and was swallowed whole by a great fish. Prophet Yūnus ﷺ knew that the terrible storm and the fish were Allāh's punishment for abandoning his mission. He was regretful and prayed to Allāh ﷻ for forgiveness. Allāh ﷻ did forgive him and caused the fish to throw him out onto the seashore.

When Prophet Yūnus ﷺ had recovered, he went back to his people and preached to them again. This time, his people believed him and a hundred thousand or more accepted his teachings.

The lesson from the story of Prophet Yūnus ﷺ teaches us never to run away from our duties or give up hope and become angry, if we don't succeed in our mission. Only Allāh ﷻ knows when success will come, and it may be nearer than we think.

# Prophet Dāwūd ﷺ

The Israelites settled in Canaan at last, and after some years, they had a king named Talut. The Israelites fought many battles with the pagan tribes in Canaan under Tālūt. One of these tribes sent a great army to attack Tālūt's small army of Israelites. Some of the army's men stayed behind, because they did not want to fight such a big army.

The enemy army had a great fighter named Jalūt who was a very big man. He came out with his sword and armor and called on any of the Israelite soldiers to come out and fight him. When he saw that nobody would fight him, he laughed at the Israelites.

Among the Israelites was a youth named Dāwūd ﷺ. He was a shepherd boy who looked after a flock of sheep and was considered too small to join the army. But he was very clever at using a sling to shoot stones. To everyone's surprise, it was young Dāwūd ﷺ who stepped out and said he would fight Jalūt.

Jalūt came forward to kill Dāwūd ﷺ with his sword, but Dāwūd ﷺ used his sling and hit Jalūt on the head with a stone. He fell to the ground and before he could recover, Dāwūd ﷺ took Jalūt's sword and killed him.

The sudden death of Jalūt encouraged the Israelite army to run into battle. The enemy was conquered. King Talut loved Prophet Dāwūd ﷺ very much for his bravery, wisdom and his beautiful singing. He gave Prophet Dāwūd ﷺ his daughter in marriage, and when Tālūt died, Prophet Dāwūd ﷺ became king.

Prophet Dāwūd ﷺ was not only a king but also a prophet. Through the angels, Allāh ﷻ revealed some beautiful songs to Dāwūd ﷺ that praised Allāh ﷻ and admired His Creations. These songs were written down. The Revelation to Prophet Dāwūd ﷺ is called the *Zabūr*.

The Israelites were very happy with their king, who led them with wisdom and justice and who never forgot that the kingdom belonged to Allāh ﷻ.

After the death of Prophet Dāwūd ﷺ, his son Prophet Sulaimān ﷺ became king, and his story follows.

# Prophet Sulaimān ﷺ

Prophet Sulaimān ﷺ grew up with all the good qualities of his father, Dāwūd ﷺ . He had his father's wisdom. Whenever he judged any case, his judgment was so fair that people were amazed. When Prophet Sulaimān ﷺ grew up and became king, his people loved and respected him as their leader.

Allāh ﷻ chose Sulaimān ﷺ as a prophet, and gave him a special gift: Prophet Sulaimān ﷺ was able to understand the language of animals. One day, Prophet Sulaimān ﷺ was leading his army through a valley in which there were many ants. Prophet Sulaimān ﷺ heard one ant say to another: "Sulaimān and his army are coming! Get back to the nests quickly or they will trample us without even noticing!" Prophet Sulaimān ﷺ heard this and smiled at the ant's words. He prayed that he would always be grateful for Allāh's favors and do right.

It was through the report of a bird, the hoopoe, that Prophet Sulaimān ﷺ heard news of the rich and powerful kingdom of Saba' in southwestern Arabia, ruled over by a queen. Its people were worshipping the sun instead of Allāh ﷻ.

Prophet Sulaimān ﷺ sent a letter to the Queen of Saba', calling her and her people to the Truth (submission to Allāh ﷻ). The Queen decided not to go to war with Prophet Sulaimān ﷺ over the issue, but instead, wanted to establish a peaceful coexistence by sending him a gift. However, this was not what Prophet Sulaimān ﷺ wanted. He had no need for more worldly goods; he only wanted to see the Queen's heart opened to the truth. When the Queen learned how her gift was received with displeasure, she set out to meet Prophet Sulaimān ﷺ face to face.

Upon her arrival at Prophet Sulaimān's palace, he treated her with honor and tested her to see if she would recognize the truth. Although she had grown up as a polytheist, she was a person who could quickly grasp the truth, so her spiritual awakening came at once. She declared that her earlier beliefs had been false and that she now submitted with Prophet Sulaimān ﷺ to the Sustainer of all of the worlds.

Although Prophet Sulaimān ﷺ and his kingdom were very rich, he always remembered and obeyed Allāh ﷻ. He never forgot his duty as a prophet to guide his people on Allāh's path. Allāh ﷻ gave him what is good in this world and will give him again what is good in the next world.

# Prophet 'Isā ﷺ

The Kingdom of the Israelites (or the Jews as they were later called) lasted a long time, but after some centuries, the Romans conquered their kingdom. The Romans ruled most of Europe, North Africa and the land of Palestine. They believed in many gods and worshipped many idols. They allowed the Jews to practice their religion, but the Jews hated to be ruled by the Roman idol-worshippers.

Prophet 'Isā's mother's name was Maryam. She was a very good woman and she often prayed to Allāh ﷻ. One day, an angel appeared to her and told her she would soon give birth to a son. She asked him: "How can I have a son, when I have no husband, and I am not a loose woman?" The angel answered that Allāh ﷻ had ordained it so and that her son would be a benefactor of mankind.

When 'Isā ﷺ was born, Maryam was alone, with no one to help her or feed her. She lived on water from a stream and fruit from a palm tree until she was strong enough to go back to her people.

When Maryam took her baby to her people, they were shocked, pointing out that her parents were not immoral people. Maryam merely pointed to the infant 'Isā ﷺ, who spoke and proclaimed himself a servant of Allāh ﷻ destined to be a prophet.

Prophet 'Isā ﷺ grew up and began preaching to his people. Allāh ﷻ gave him the gift of beautiful speech. He could use simple stories to help people understand sometimes difficult concepts. 'Isā ﷺ taught them that they should obey Allāh's laws and love one another. Allāh ﷻ also gave him the gift of healing the sick. 'Isā ﷺ soon became famous. Often, the blind, the lame and the sick used to come to him, so that he could pray to Allāh ﷻ to make them well. One day, he was asked to bring a dead man back to life. By Allāh ﷻ's power, the man lived again.

Allāh ﷻ also gave Prophet ʿĪsā ﷺ a revelation called the *Injīl*, as He had given the *Tawrāt* to Prophet Mūsa ﷺ and the *Zabūr* to Prophet Dāwūd ﷺ .

Many people began to follow Prophet ʿĪsā ﷺ , but the Jewish priests and religious leaders did not like it. They were angry that this young man was becoming a popular leader and teacher. They had studied the Holy Books and read the Jewish laws and considered themselves the chosen experts. Prophet ʿĪsā ﷺ proved that they loved their positions as priests and leaders more than they loved Allāh ﷻ.

Their jealousy moved them to plan his death. They told the Roman Governor of Palestine that Prophet ʿĪsā ﷺ was a rebel. They said that he was gathering followers so that he would be made king of the Jews. Then he would fight the Romans and drive them out of Palestine. The Roman Governor agreed that Prophet ʿĪsā ﷺ should be put to death on a cross.

However, it was not Allāh's Will that His beloved Prophet ʿĪsā ﷺ be killed. He saved ʿĪsā ﷺ from death, as He had saved other prophets before him when they were in danger.

Some of the people who later followed Prophet ʿĪsā ﷺ claimed that Allāh ﷻ was the father of ʿĪsā ﷺ , and that ʿĪsā ﷺ was also God. However, the Qurʿan tells us that this is not true because Prophet ʿĪsā ﷺ, like all the other prophets, taught people to worship only the Allāh ﷻ. We know that Allāh ﷻ has no sons or daughters and that every human being was made by Him and is His servant. Muslims respect and love ʿĪsā ﷺ as a prophet and messenger. Therefore, when we mention Prophet ʿĪsā ﷺ, we always say: "May the peace of Allāh be with him," as we do for all the prophets.

WE HAVE LEARNED:

* All the ancient prophets and messengers taught that Allāh ﷻ is one.
* They lived their lives as and example for us and all believers.
* Most people didn't care to listen to what they had to say and even fought against them.

# LESSON 3

---

## THE LIFE OF PROPHET MUHAMMAD ﷺ

### Birth and Youth

Prophet Muhammad (Rasūlullāh ﷺ) was born about 570 years after the birth of Prophet ʿIsā ﷺ . He became an orphan at a very young age. His father died before his birth, and his mother died when he was only six years old. His grandfather, Abdul Muttalib, took the responsibility of caring for him, but he also died two years later. Then Rasūlullāh's uncle, Abu Talib, became his guardian. As a young boy, Rasūlullāh ﷺ looked after a flock of sheep near Makkah.

Makkah is the city in Arabia, which had developed from the place where Ibrāhīm ﷺ had taken his wife Hajar and baby Ismaʿil ﷺ many hundreds years earlier. It is also the site where Ibrāhīm ﷺ and Ismaʿil ﷺ had built the *Ka'bah* as a place of worship for Allāh ﷻ. But after some time, the people of that area began to worship many gods, filling the *Ka'bah* with idols. Idol-worshippers from all over Arabia used to come there for pilgrimages. Makkah became an important trading town between Southern Arabia and Syria to the north.

When Rasūlullāh ﷺ was old enough, his uncle, Abū Tālib, took him on some of his trading journeys. He went as far north as Syria, where he saw mountains and rivers, and people of many different races.

Abū Tālib loved his nephew, Muhammad ﷺ, very much. Everyone respected Muhammad ﷺ for his honesty and good character. He was given the title of "Al-Amīn", "the trustworthy."

## Work as a Trader

Rasūlullāh ﷺ learned to manage trading caravans by helping his uncle, Abū Tālib. He took a job with the trading caravan of a rich and respected widow named Khadījah ؓ. She liked his honesty and good work and soon appointed him as manager of her trading caravan.

## Marriage to Khadījah ؓ

Khadījah ؓ was so impressed by Rasūlullāh ﷺ's character that she proposed to marry him, and he accepted the proposal. It was a very happy marriage.

So, the orphan had grown up to become a successful man, with a good wife and children. But this was not the end of Rasūlullāh's destiny. Allāh ﷻ had greater plans for him.

## Search for the Truth

Rasūlullāh ﷺ was still not happy. All the comforts and good things of this world, which he now possessed, did not satisfy him. He felt restless. He used to go off alone to think about the mysteries of the universe and life. What was it all for?

The people of Makkah said: "We live and we die. Let us be merry before we enter the grave." To please themselves, they did many wrong deeds. They used to drink and dance and fight. They collected wealth by any means and cheated people to become rich. They treated their slaves badly. They had no respect for women. If a female was born, they often used to bury her alive. They worshipped idols that they believed could help them in their affairs.

All these things disillusioned Rasūlullāh 鷺. How could an idol, made by human hands, help anyone? He was very curious about the existence of the universe. He often asked himself, "What kind of god is it who could make the earth and all the stars in the sky? He wondered if he, too, would live and die like the others, without knowing the answers to these questions.

## The First Revelation

The answers to his questions suddenly came one night when Rasūlullāh 鷺 was in the Cave of *Hirā'* on the Mount of Mercy, where he often went and sat alone to think.

The Angel Jibrīl appeared before him and held him in his arms. The angel squeezed him hard and then commanded him: "*Iqra'*! (Read!)." As he had no formal education, Rasūlullāh 鷺 replied: "I cannot read!" The angel squeezed him again and commanded him to read. Rasūlullāh 鷺 again answered: "I cannot read!" The angel squeezed him a third time and commanded: "Read in the name of your Lord, Who created, created man from a clot of blood. Read! And your Lord is Most Bountiful, Who taught man the use of the pen, taught him what he knew not" (i.e. the first five verses of *Sūrah* 96, *Al-'Alaq*). The angel then introduced himself Angel Jibrīl . He informed the frightened forty-year-old man that he was chosen to be Rasūlullāh 鷺 , the Messenger of Allāh 鷺.

# Preaching in Makkah

Rasūlullāh ﷺ felt comforted when Khadījah ﷺ believed him, and he later told several of his relatives and close friends what had happened.

After some time, the Revelations came more and more frequently. Through them, Allāh ﷻ told Rasūlullāh ﷺ to teach his people that He, Allāh ﷻ, is the One God, alone and without partner, the Creator of heaven and earth. Rasūlullāh ﷺ was told to teach people that life does not end with death. On the Day of Judgment, Allāh ﷻ will give life to every dead creature. They will all be judged for their actions on earth and rewarded or punished accordingly. Rasūlullāh ﷺ was asked by Allāh ﷻ to teach people that they should prepare themselves for judgment not by drinking and dancing, but by maintaining good behavior. They should care for the weak and needy by giving freely from their wealth. They should not cheat and quarrel with each other. They should be kind and generous to their wives and to their parents. Above all, they must stop worshipping the stone and wood idols.

A few people agreed with what Rasūlullāh ﷺ taught and believed. They accepted the message of Islām. However, most of the people laughed at him. They said he was insane, or that he was a poet composing verses, or a liar. They did not like him to say that their idols had no power to help or harm. Yet, he continued patiently to persuade them.

Allāh ﷻ then instructed Rasūlullāh ﷺ to preach Islām openly. More people began to join him. The leaders of Makkah then became worried about their trade. Many people came to Makkah to worship the idols at the *Ka'bah*. As Allāh ﷻ's religion spread through Rasūlullāh ﷺ, they feared the idols would be destroyed, and people would stop coming to Makkah as pilgrims and traders.

## The Persecution

Therefore, a great number of the people of Makkah decided to stop the spread of Islām by attacking the Muslims. They punished those who were weak, especially the slaves. Some were beaten, while others were killed. Those who had powerful relatives to protect them were abused or were tortured by different means. When Rasūlullāh ﷺ prayed at the *Ka'bah* in public, some people used to throw filthy things over him. But he endured it patiently, knowing that he was doing what Allāh ﷻ had told him to do. At one time, Rasūlullāh ﷺ sent some of his weaker followers across the sea to Ethiopia to escape the persecution of the idolworshippers in Makkah.

The leaders of Makkah decided to drive the Muslims out of town. Nobody was allowed to visit them or trade with them. They were short of food. Life became very hard for them. Because of these hardships, Rasūlullāh's dear wife <u>Kh</u>adījah ﷺ died. Soon after, his uncle, Abū Tālib, who had always protected him against the leaders of Makkah, also died.

## The Hijrah

At last, there came a new hope for the Muslims from Allāh ﷻ. Many of the people of Madinah (then called Yathrib) had become Muslims, and they now invited Rasūlullāh ﷺ to come to Madinah as their leader.

Rasūlullāh ﷺ made arrangements for the other Muslims of Makkah to leave first. They left quietly, a few at a time, and traveled to Madinah. When all those who wanted to go had gone, Rasūlullāh ﷺ also left Makkah quietly, leaving his young cousin, 'Alī ﷺ, behind to sleep on his bed as a decoy.

That night, the leaders of Makkah planned to kill Rasūlullāh ﷺ. When the men broke into his house, they found ʿAli ؓ there, sleeping on his bed. They did not want to kill ʿAli ؓ, only Rasūlullāh ﷺ. so they left to go find him. In this way, Rasūlullāh ﷺ was saved and protected by Allāh ﷻ.

Rasūlullāh ﷺ traveled with his old friend, Abū Bakr ؓ, across the mountains and desert toward Madinah. The enemies sent horsemen to kill them, but Rasūlullāh ﷺ took refuge in a cave. The horsemen came to search the cave, but when they saw that a spider had spun a web across the entrance and that a dove sat undisturbed on a nest close by, they thought: "There can be nobody inside," so they went away. Rasūlullāh ﷺ and Abū Bakr ؓ then resumed their journey, until they finally reached Madinah safely.

## The New State in Madinah

The Muslims of Madinah welcomed the Muslims who arrived from Makkah wholeheartedly. Those who came from Makkah had brought nothing with them. They had to leave behind their houses and property. So, each person or family stayed with a Madinan family, until they were able to get a house and look after themselves.

Rasūlullāh ﷺ built a mosque and a house. Then, he began to organize Madinah in the Islāmic way. Allāh ﷻ continued to guide him through periodic revelations.

The Revelations continued for a period of twenty-three years.

Whenever a new Revelation came, Rasūlullāh ﷺ ordered that scribes should write it down. The Revelations were memorized by many of the Muslims and the written versions were kept. They form the Qur'ān, the Holy Book of the Muslims.

The Muslims were directed by Allāh ﷻ to organize prayer five times a day, so that they would always remember Him. They were directed to fast throughout the month of Ramadan. They were directed to give *Zakāh* as charity to the poor and needy and help the cause of Islām. The bad customs of the idol-worshippers (such as the burial of live baby girls) were forbidden, and the people began to lead their lives in accordance with the *Shari'ah* (Allāh's law). But, the Muslims could not go on pilgrimage, because Makkah was in the hands of the idol-worshippers, who did not allow them to enter the city.

## The Battle of Badr

Over the next few years, there was a continuous struggle between the Muslims and the idol-worshippers of Makkah. Several important battles took place. The first was the Battle of Badr, two years after the *Hijrah,* in which Rasūlullāh's small army of about 300 men defeated an army of almost 1,000 idol-worshippers from Makkah.

## The Battle of Uḥud

The people of Makkah were shocked at being defeated by such a small group of Muslims at Badr. Two years later, they came back to Madinah with a much larger army. They fought the Muslims at Uḥud, just outside Madinah. The Muslims were winning the battle, when some of their soldiers disobeyed Rasūlullāh's orders. The enemies then killed many Muslims and the remaining Muslims climbed the mountains around Uḥud, to escape. The army of Makkah did not chase them to the mountains, but instead, they retreated.

## The Battle of Al-Khandaq (The Trench)

The army of Makkah again attacked Madinah in the fifth year after *Hijrah* with an army of 10,000 men, intending to destroy Madinah. Rasūlullāh ﷺ followed the advice of a Persian Muslim, named Salmān, and prepared a trench along the north of the city. Salmān arranged his 3,000 men to defend Madinah from within the trench instead of going out to fight the enemy in open battle. The people of Makkah and their Bedouin allies were not familiar with this kind of warfare. They were unable to enter Madinah and after a three-week siege, they returned home defeated.

## The Treaty of Hudaibiyya

In the sixth year after *Hijrah*, Rasūlullāh ﷺ and about 1,400 followers set out for the pilgrimage to Makkah. They stopped at Hudaibiyya, near Makkah, and made it clear to the people of Makkah that they had come for pilgrimage, not for battle. The people of Makkah were also not prepared for war, and they agreed that if Rasūlullāh ﷺ would go back, he and his followers could perform the pilgrimage the following year.

After some discussion, Rasūlullāh ﷺ made a treaty with the people of Makkah. It was called the Treaty of Hudaibiyya. One of the conditions of the treaty was that there should be no fighting between Muslims and the Makkans for ten years. This condition greatly helped the cause of Islām. Rasūlullāh ﷺ took the opportunity to send preachers to all parts of Arabia to teach people Islām, and many people became Muslims. The Muslims continued to increase in number until the Makkan idol-worshippers lost their power in the land. Rasūlullāh ﷺ also sent messages to the rulers of the great empires of Persia , Byzantium and to the Christian Patriarch of Alexandria in Egypt, inviting them to accept Islām's teachings.

## The Conquest of Makkah

Two years after the Treaty of Hudaibiyya, the idolworshippers broke the treaty and attacked the Muslim allies. In response, Rasūlullāh ﷺ sent a great army of Muslims to Makkah. When the idol-worshippers saw the size of the Muslim army, they decided not to fight. They surrendered the city to Rasūlullāh ﷺ , whom they had driven out eight years before.

## The Destruction of the Idols at the Ka'bah

Rasūlullāh ﷺ entered Makkah in peace and did not allow the Muslims to punish or harm anyone. Seeing this behavior and that Islām stood for such mercy and kindness, many citizens of Makkah embraced Islām. Rasūlullāh ﷺ went to the *Ka'bah* and ordered his followers to destroy all the idols. This was done, and the *Ka'bah* was again used as the House of Worship for the One God, as it was at the time of Prophet Ibrāhīm ﷺ . Rasūlullāh ﷺ then showed the Muslims the Islāmic way of offering pilgrimage.

By this time, most of the people in Arabia had learned about the religion of Islām, and they embraced Islām each day by the hundreds.

## The Farewell Pilgrimage

Rasūlullāh ﷺ was now sixty-three years old, and he sensed that the time had come for his return to Allāh ﷻ. He made a last pilgrimage to Makkah and spoke to his people. He told them to always be fair and just and to care for the weak. He reminded them to give women their rights and give Jews and Christians the right to practice their religions in the way to which they were accustomed.

He told them that he was leaving with them two things-the Qur'ān and his *Sunnah* (his way of life or practice). He said if the Muslims would follow the Qur'ān and *Sunnah,* they would never go astray.

Soon after this (ten years after the *Hijrah*), Rasūlullāh ﷺ passed away in his house in Madinah. He was buried there. Even today, people visit his last resting place and pray for him. May Allāh ﷻ bless Rasūlullāh ﷺ , the last of the prophets, and help the Muslims to follow the Qur'ān and the *Sunnah* for the rest of our lives.

## Rasūlūllah's Appearance and Character

Rasūlullāh ﷺ was a man of medium build and height. He was handsome, having thick black hair, a large forehead, thick eyebrows and large black eyes with long eyelashes. He had good even teeth, a thick neck, broad chest and shoulders, and lightcolored skin.

He walked in a firm manner and always appeared to be deep in thought. His character always impressed people. His trustworthiness and honesty have already been mentioned. From the records in the *Ḥadīth* of what he said and did, we know a lot more about his behavior.

He was always kindhearted, especially towards the weak. His kindness extended even to animals. He never allowed his followers to overload or ill-treat their animals, or to be cruel to wild animals. When some of his followers took some baby birds from a nest, he ordered them to return the birds to their mother. He even stopped them from destroying insects, as long as they were harmless.

His kindness also showed in his forgiveness to his enemies, as could be seen at the conquest of Makkah.

He was the best of husbands and was very fond of children. His wife, Ā'ishah, said that he was a model of what the Qur'ān teaches.

Moreover, he was very modest, both in his dress and behavior. When someone praised him as "the best of creatures," he humbly disagreed, saying: "No, that was (Prophet) Ibrāhīm."

His modesty also showed in his lifestyle, which was extremely simple. Even when he became Head of State, he had very few possessions. He used to mend his own clothes, take care of his household needs, and do his share of any physical labor with the *Ṣaḥābah* ﷺ (his companions). They urged him to let them do it for him, but he replied: "I know you could do it for me, but I hate to have any privilege over you."

There was seldom any meat or cooked food in his house. He shared the poverty of other Muslims. His wife, 'Ā'ishah ﷺ, said that sometimes they lived for months on a diet of milk and dates.

Rasūlullāh ﷺ is reported to have said:

*"My Sustainer has given me nine commands:*

    *i)     To remain conscious of Allāh ﷻ, in private or in public.*
    *ii)    To speak humbly, whether angry or pleased.*
    *iii)   To show moderation, both when poor and when rich.*
    *iv)   To reunite friendship with those who have broken it off with me.*
    *v)    To give to him who refuses me.*
    *vi)   To forgive him who has wronged me.*
    *vii)   That my silence should be filled with thought.*
    *viii)  That my looking should be an admonition.*
    *ix)   That I should command what is right."*

This was indeed how he behaved, and this is the beautiful and inspiring example that every Muslim would like to emulate.

## WE HAVE LEARNED:

* Rasūlullāh ﷺ was chosen by Allāh ﷻ to be the very last messenger to mankind.
* Despite all the suffering he had to endure, Rasūlullāh ﷺ never lost his faith in Allāh ﷻ.
* All Muslims must love Rasūlullāh ﷺ with all of their hearts.

# LESSON 4

## THE FOUR RIGHTLY-GUIDED KHULAFĀ'

### The Four Rightly-Guided *Khulafā'*

The four rightly-guided *Khulafā'* were Abū Bakr ﷺ, 'Umar ﷺ, 'Uthman ﷺ and 'Ali ﷺ . They were all close companions ( *Ṣaḥābah* ﷺ) of Rasūlullāh ﷺ.

Khalifah was the title given to the leaders of the Muslims after the death of Rasūlullāh ﷺ. The first four *Khulafā'* were called rightly-guided because they faithfully followed the Qur'ān and the *Sunnah* in their behavior and way of government.  The Muslims chose the four rightly-guided *Khulafā'*, because they were good Muslims and wise leaders. After these four *Khulafā*, the leadership was either taken by force or passed from father to son.

### Abu Bakr ﷺ, the First *Khalīfah*

Abū Bakr ﷺ  was about three years younger than Rasūlullāh ﷺ , and was his close friend from childhood. He grew up to be a trader and was quite rich. People admired him for his good behavior and his kindness towards the poor and the weak.

He was one of the earliest people to accept Islām, and he taught Islām to others. He used his money to free Muslim slaves who were being punished by their masters because of their religion. Bilal ﷺ was one of the slaves he freed.

Abū Bakr ﷺ gave Rasūlullāh ﷺ his daughter ‘Ā’i<u>sh</u>ah ﷺ in marriage. When Rasūlullāh ﷺ migrated to Madinah, it was Abū Bakr ﷺ who accompanied him on that dangerous journey. He also fought alongside the Prophet in the battles against the idolworshippers.

When Rasūlullāh ﷺ died, many people refused to believe it. But Abū Bakr ﷺ spoke to the crowd saying: "O people, whoever worshipped Muhammad, know that Muhammad is indeed dead. But whoever worshipped Allāh, Allāh is alive and will never die."

Abū Bakr ﷺ was chosen as the new leader of the Muslims. He promised to help the weak and obey Allāh ﷻ and His Prophet .

He lived in a simple way, as Rasūlullāh ﷺ had done. His clothes were plain, and he always liked to do his own work with his own hands, without slaves or servants to attend to him.

During his Caliphate, he fought successfully against false prophets and others who tried to break up the Muslim ‘*Ummah* ("community of believers").

When he was forced to fight, he ordered his soldiers as follows: "Do not run away from battle or disobey orders. Do not kill an old man, a woman or a child. Do not harm date palms or cut down fruit trees. Do not slaughter any sheep, cows or camels except for food. You will meet people who spend their lives in monasteries (i.e. Christian monks); leave them alone, and do not disturb them."

Abū Bakr ﷺ was a kindhearted man, but he defended Islām firmly and faithfully and was loved by his people.

# 'Umar ﷺ, the Second *Khalīfah*

'Umar ﷺ was about thirteen years younger than Rasūlullāh ﷺ. He was active and intelligent and he learned as a child how to read and write. He was good at public speaking, wrestling and fighting with a sword. He was a trader and visited many lands and saw many kinds of people.

When Rasūlullāh ﷺ began to spread the message of Islām, 'Umar ﷺ opposed him at first. When his servant became a Muslim, he beat her until he was too tired to go on. One day, he decided to kill Rasūlullāh ﷺ and moved towards his house. On the way, he met a friend who told him that his ('Umar's) sister and her husband had already become Muslims. 'Umar ﷺ went straight to her house and found her reading from the Qur'ān. He slapped her, causing her to bleed, but she told him: " 'Umar ﷺ, you can do what you like, but you cannot turn our hearts away from Islām."

'Umar ﷺ was surprised at her bravery and ashamed that he had hurt his sister. He asked her to show him what she was reading. When he read the verses of the Qur'ān, he at once saw the truth in them. He went to Rasūlullāh's house and accepted Islām.

'Umar ﷺ was bold and fearless, and he gave courage to the other Muslims in Makkah.

Rasūlullāh ﷺ trusted him as a close companion. Later in Madinah, 'Umar ﷺ gave his widowed daughter, Hafsah, to Rasūlullāh ﷺ in marriage.

When Abū Bakr ﷺ died, 'Umar ﷺ was chosen as the second

*Khalīfah*. Under his leadership, *Islām* spread to both the east and west. Because he was merciful and generous to nonMuslims, many of them embraced *Islām*.

'Umar ⬥ refused to live like a king with wealth and a show of power. He once told a group of governors: "Remember, I have not appointed you to rule over your people, but to serve them. You should set an example with your good conduct, so that people may follow you."

He wore such simple clothes that visitors could not tell he was the *Khalīfah*. It is said that when 'Umar ⬥ went to Jerusalem, he traveled with one assistant and a camel, each taking turns riding the camel. When they reached Jerusalem, it was the assistant's turn to ride the camel. The Christians of Jerusalem were amazed at 'Umar's spirit of brotherhood.

'Umar ⬥ often went into the streets at night to find out what people were really thinking and to understand their problems. He was never too proud to be corrected if he was wrong. One day, a woman corrected him publicly in the mosque of Madinah (about the amount of dowry). 'Umar ⬥ accepted her criticism, saying: "The woman is right and 'Umar ⬥ is wrong."

'Umar ⬥ made the government work for the people. They built new cities, roads and canals. The poor and needy were cared for from the *Zakāh* funds. Christians and Jews were free to practice their religion.

By the time 'Umar ⬥ died, the world of *Islām* had spread to the west across most of North Africa and to the east as far as the borders of India and China.

'Umar ⬥ never kept guards, because he wanted no barriers to come between him and his people. One unfortunate day, a slave wounded him with a knife in the mosque. He died three days later.

## 'Uthman ﷺ, the Third Khalifah

'Uthman ﷺ was a friend of Abū Bakr ﷺ. It was Abū Bakr ﷺ who introduced him to *Islām*. 'Uthman ﷺ could read and write and became a successful trader.

However, he was one of those Muslims whom the idol-worshippers punished. He had to leave with the group of Muslims who went to Abyssinia for safety. Later, he returned and joined Rasūlullāh ﷺ in Madinah.

Rasūlullāh ﷺ gave 'Uthman his daughter, Ruqayyah, in marriage. However, she died just before the Battle of Badr. Uthman ﷺ was so sad that Rasūlullāh ﷺ then gave him the hand of his other daughter, Umm Kulthum.

On the death of 'Umar ﷺ, 'Uthman ﷺ was chosen as *Khalīfah*. One of his most important official acts was the order to make authentic copies of the Qur'ān, and send them to each important city in the Muslim world for safekeeping. This made it impossible for anyone to change the words of the Qur'ān. To this day, the Qur'ān remains unchanged.

'Uthman ﷺ had the good qualities expected from a Muslim leader: kindness, honesty, generosity and modesty. He was very pious and knew the meaning of the Qur'ān very well.

He was, however, an old man of nearly seventy when he became *Khalīfah*. He could not match 'Umar in strength and energy to control the government of the Muslim world, which now covered a very large part of the earth. Some people were not happy with his government. One night, a group of dissidents, murdered him in his home while he was reading the Qur'ān.

## 'Ali , the Fourth Khalifah

'Ali was the son of Abū Tālib, Rasūlullāh 's uncle. When Rasūlullāh grew up, Abū Tālib sent 'Ali to live with him. In Rasūlullāh 's house, 'Ali learned from the best example of piety, good manners and conduct.

'Ali was only ten years old when Rasūlullāh received the first Revelation. Rasūlullāh invited him to accept *Islām*, and 'Ali became the first youth to become Muslim.

Rasūlullāh invited his relatives to a meal and told them about his message. He asked them all: "Who will join me in the cause of Allāh ?" Nobody spoke, until 'Ali stood up and said: "I am the youngest of all present here. My eyes trouble me, because they are sore, and my legs are thin and weak, but I will join you and help you in any way I can." The others laughed at him, but 'Ali kept his promise and helped Rasūlullāh through all sorts of danger with great bravery.

When Rasūlullāh left Makkah for Madinah, it was 'Ali who dared to stay in Rasūlullāh's bed while Rasūlullāh left for Madinah. When the people of Makkah discovered that it was 'Ali and not Rasūlullāh , they were very angry.

'Ali ﷺ joined Rasūlullāh ﷺ in Madinah and fought in almost every battle against the idol-worshippers. It was said that at the Battle of Uḥud, he had been wounded sixteen times.

Rasūlullāh ﷺ gave 'Ali ﷺ his beloved daughter, Fatimah ﷺ, in marriage. The two of them became the parents of Ḥasan ﷺ and Ḥusain ﷺ.

'Ali ﷺ followed Rasūlullāh ﷺ in his simple way of life. He was so generous that at times, his own family went hungry.

He had great knowledge of the Qur'ān and the Arabic language. Many of his wise sayings, speeches and letters have been preserved. He was fearless and brave in battle, but he took no pleasure in fighting and made peace whenever possible. All his good qualities and abilities were combined to form a sincere and modest manner.

The Muslim world, however, was still not at peace. The fourth *Khalīfah*, 'Ali ﷺ, was killed by one of his enemies when he was praying in the mosque.

After the time of Abū Bakr ﷺ, 'Umar ﷺ, 'Uthman ﷺ and 'Ali ﷺ, the *Khulafā'* behaved in a different way. They wanted to keep the Caliphate in their family, so their main goal was to pass it from father to son. Some of the *Khulafā'* were good, but most of them had forgotten the way Rasūlullāh ﷺ and the righteous *Khulafā'* had ruled. They accumulated wealth and lived in luxurious palaces with fine clothes and food. They enjoyed living as kings in this world and often forgot about Allāh ﷻ, the King of the whole universe, and about the Day of Judgment.

Rasūlullāh ﷺ said:

*The best of rulers is he who loves his people and whose people love him; who prays for his people and whose people pray for him.*
(Transmitted by Muslim)

May Allāh ﷻ bless the Muslims with such good leaders again.

WE HAVE LEARNED:

* After Rasūlullāh ﷺ, Muslims have had the *Khulafā'* to lead them.
* The best of the *Khulafā'* were the first four: Abū Bakr ﷺ, 'Umar ﷺ, 'Uthman ﷺ and 'Ali ﷺ .
* They devoted their whole lives to the cause of *Islām*.

# LESSON 5

---

## OTHER FAMOUS MUSLIMS

We have learned about four of the most famous Ṣaḥābah 🕮 of Rasūlullāh 🕮: Abū Bakr 🕮, 'Umar 🕮, 'Uthman 🕮 and 'Ali 🕮. However, it was not only the men who became famous through their deeds as Muslims. Many women devotedly served Islām as well. Furthermore, not all of Rasūlullāh's companions were Arabs. We shall now hear how Khadījah 🕮 and 'Ā'ishah 🕮 (two of Rasūlullāh's wives), Fāṭimah 🕮 (his daughter) and Bilāl 🕮 (an African slave), became famous in the history of Islām.

### Khadījah 🕮 bint Khuwailid

Khadījah 🕮 was a noble and respected widow who lived in Makkah. She owned a trading business, which she managed herself. She then appointed Rasūlullāh 🕮 to work for her.

When she saw his good, honest work, she appointed him manager. In due course, she proposed to marry him, and he accepted. She was the epitome of understanding and true goodness of character. She offered to marry him despite the difference in their economic and social background. She was forty years old, while Rasūlullāh 🕮 was only twenty-five, but because she was a very good wife and he the best of husbands, they were very happy together. Khadījah 🕮 had six children with him, among whom was his beloved daughter, Fāṭimah 🕮.

When Rasūlullāh ﷺ became restless and went off into the mountains to think, she understood his need to do so and supported his actions. On the night when he first saw the angel in the Cave of *Hirā'*, Rasūlullāh ﷺ returned home trembling with fear. He told Khadījah ﷺ what had happened. It was Khadījah ﷺ who held him in her arms and told him she sincerely believed that he was neither mad nor misled, but blessed to be chosen as a Messenger of Allāh ﷻ.

She comforted him and supported him throughout those years in Makkah when he was laughed at, abūsed and attacked by the idol-worshippers.

She gladly gave her wealth for the cause of *Islām* and suffered with him up until her death. Rasūlullāh ﷺ told her she would be one of the most honored women in Paradise.

As long as she lived, he never married another woman, and even long after her death, he spoke of her with great love and respect. Just before the *Hijrah*, she died in his arms at the age of sixty-three.

Her life shows how important it is for a man to have a loving and understanding wife with whom he can share life's joys and sorrows. Without peace and support from his wife, it would not have been easy for the Prophet s to face the sort of hardship and suffering he faced while he preached among the idolworshippers in Makkah.

## 'Ā'ishah bint Abū Bakr ﷺ

'Ā'ishah ﷺ was the daughter of Abū Bakr ﷺ, Rasūlullāh's close friend.

When Rasūlullāh's first wife <u>Kh</u>adījah 🕮 died, Rasūlullāh 🕮 felt very sad. Abū Bakr 🕮 loved Rasūlullāh 🕮 very much and felt his pain. So, Abū Bakr 🕮 offered him his daughter in marriage.

'Ā'ishah 🕮 was still young at the time. She was a lively, intelligent girl, and Rasūlullāh 🕮 loved her and enjoyed her company. He liked to entertain her by playing games. Sometimes, she won and sometimes, he did.

She learned much about Islām from Rasūlullāh 🕮 and used to question him often about matters of religion. When she learned something, she never forgot it. She was also a good speaker. Because of these qualities, she became an important person in the community and even before Rasūlullāh 🕮's death, people used to come to her and ask questions about Islām. Rasūlullāh 🕮 was pleased with her intelligence and said to his people: "You can get half your religion from 'Ā'ishah."

Besides providing Rasūlullāh 🕮 companionship at home with love and care, 'Ā'ishah 🕮 often accompanied him on journeys and expeditions.

When Rasūlullāh 🕮 felt that his death was near, he asked to be taken to 'Ā'ishah's apartment next to the mosque. There she nursed him until the last moment, and he died in her arms. He was buried at the very place where he died, and what was 'Ā'ishah's apartment, is now part of Masjid-un-Nabi in Madinah.

After Rasūlullāh's death, 'Ā'ishah 🕮 maintained her position of respect among the Muslims. She used to teach other women. Both men and women came to her to learn what Rasūlullāh 🕮 had said and

215

how he behaved. In this way, she became one of the most important reporters of *Hadīth* (the tradition of Rasūlullāh ﷺ).

Her life shows how a Muslim woman can use her intelligence and scholarship to make a great contribution to the cause of *Islām*. It also shows how, like Khadījah ﷺ before her, 'Ā'ishah ﷺ was able to give Rasūlullāh ﷺ the love and understanding that helped him through all of those years of struggle and fighting after the *Hijrah* to Madinah.

## Fatimah bint Muhammad ﷺ

Fātimah ﷺ, the beloved daughter of Rasūlullāh ﷺ, was born in Makkah, eight years before the *Hijrah*. She was the fourth and youngest daughter of her mother, Khadījah ﷺ .

She was brought up under the care of the greatest teacher of mankind and the kindest mother. She looked very much like her father and she also possessed his saintly character. At the time of her mother's death, Fātimah ﷺ was still a child. Because of the loss, she became even more devoted to her father. He loved her very much and spoke about her on several occasions. He is reported to have said: "Fātimah ﷺ is my child. One who distresses her, distresses me, and one who comforts her, comforts me."

On another occasion, he said: "O Fātimah! Allāh will not like a person who displeases you and will be pleased with a person who wins your favor." Rasūlullāh's wife, 'Ā'ishah ﷺ said, after the death of Khadījah ﷺ : "I have never come across a greater personality than that of Fātimah except that of her father, Allāh's Messenger ."

Fātimah 🌹 was a serious child. She was physically weak and did not enjoy good health. Thus, she did not indulge much in playing with other children. Under her father's guidance and inspiration, she grew up to be an unselfish young woman, who always had sympathy towards the sufferings of others.

When she was eighteen-years old, 'Ali 🌹, Rasūlullāh's cousin, sought her hand in marriage and Rasūlullāh 🌹 agreed. They were married at a simple ceremony. Rasūlullāh 🌹 told her: "My daughter, I have married you to a person who has stronger faith and is more learned than others and one who is distinguished for his morality and virtues."

Fātimah 🌹 and 'Ali's household was hardworking, pious and generous. Fātimah 🌹 never had a servant to help her in spite of her weakness and poor health. Often they and their family went hungry because they had given away most of what they had to the poor. Fātimah 🌹 had five children, among whom were Ḥasan 🌹 and Ḥusain 🌹, Rasūlullāh 🌹's beloved grandsons.

Fātimah 🌹 lived for only six months after the death of Rasūlullāh 🌹. She died at the age of twenty-eight and was buried amidst universal mourning.

The personality of Fātimah 🌹 was free of selfish desires and false pride. Rasūlullāh 🌹 proclaimed her: "the Queen of women in Paradise."

## Bilal Ibn Rabāḥ 🌹

Bilāl 🌹 was the first African to accept *Islām*. He was born a slave in Makkah, and grew up to be tall, strong and handsome. He was also honest, wise and capable. Because of these qualities, his master put him in charge of his caravan. It was on such a journey that he became a close friend of Abū Bakr 🙵, not long before Rasūlullāh 🙵 had his first Revelation.

When Rasūlullāh 🙵 told Abū Bakr 🙵 about his Revelation, Abū Bakr 🙵 accepted *Islām* and at once began to tell his friends about this religion. Bilāl 🙵 was the first of them who embraced *Islām* immediately. At first, he kept this a secret; as a slave, he had no right to change his beliefs and therefore, could be punished by his master. However, someone told his master about his conversion. His master was very angry with him and beat Bilāl 🙵 to make him give up *Islām*. But, Bilāl 🙵 refused. Then, his master took him to the desert and made him lie in the hot sun, wearing a metal dress. But Bilāl 🙵 would only repeat *"Ahad! Ahad!"* meaning: One (God), One (God). Then, his master put a huge stone on his chest. The pain was terrible, but Bilāl 🙵 still repeated *"Ahad! Ahad!"* and said he would rather die than go back to their religion. Before he could torture him to death, Abū Bakr 🙵 arrived and asked them if he could buy Bilāl 🙵. They asked for a high price, expecting Abū Bakr 🙵 to refuse, but he agreed. So Bilāl 🙵 was saved, and Abū Bakr 🙵 set him free from slavery.

Bilāl 🙵 later emigrated with the Muslims to Madinah and lived in Abū Bakr's house attached to the Mosque. Rasūlullāh 🙵 appointed him as the first *Mu'adhin* (one who does the call for prayer), because he had a beautiful and powerful voice. He also placed him in charge of the Treasury from which money was used to help the poor and to take care of guests.

When Makkah surrendered to Rasūlullāh 🙵, Bilāl 🙵 was one of those who entered the *Ka'bah* with Rasūlullāh 🙵 to destroy the idols. With this task done, Rasūlullāh 🙵 asked Bilāl 🙵 to climb on the roof of the *Ka'bah* and call the *'Adhan* (call to prayer) while 'Ali 🕊 and others destroyed the idols outside the *Ka'bah*.

Bilāl 🕊 fought in every battle at the side of Rasūlullāh 🕊, and remained Abū Bakr's close friend.

When Rasūlullāh 🕊 died, Bilāl 🕊 felt so sad that he could not call the *'Adhan* again from Rasūlullāh's Mosque, and a new *Mu'adhin* was appointed. Bilāl 🕊 called the *'Adhan* again on only two occasions: once at the request of 'Umar 🕊 at the site of Prophet Sulaimān's temple in Jerusalem, and once in Madinah at the request of Rasūlullāh's grandsons, Ḥasan 🕊 and Ḥusain 🕊.

When Abū Bakr 🕊 died two years after Rasūlullāh 🕊, Bilāl 🕊 decided to leave Madinah and joined the Muslim army in Syria. The rest of his life (eight years) was spent in *Jihād*. He died peacefully in Damascus.

Bilāl's greatest qualities were his sincerity of faith, bravery, honesty and his loyalty to Rasūlullāh 🕊 and his friends. His story also shows how a man of humble origins an African slave rose to become one of the great heroes among Muslims only because of his belief in Islām. He proved that in the brotherhood of Islām, all men are equal.


WE HAVE LEARNED:

    * Rasūlullāh 🕊 had many *Ṣahābah* 🕊, whose lives were greatly
      affected by him.
    * Many women had a large role to play in the life of Rasūlullāh 🕊.
    * Every Muslim should love all of the *Ṣahābah* 🕊 of
      Rasūlullāh 🕊.

# LESSON 6

---

## THE FOUNDERS OF THE
## FOUR SCHOOLS OF JURISPRUDENCE

There are four great Muslim *'Ālims* (scholars) whose names should be known by every Muslim. They were great scholars who studied the Qur'ān and *Ḥadīth* in great depth. From their understanding based on their lifetime's work, unified systems covering all aspects of Islāmic law were established.

The four most famous *Fuqaha* (jurists) in Islāmic history were Imām Abū Ḥanīfah, Imām Mālik ibn 'Anas, Imām Ash-Shāfi'i and Imām Aḥmad ibn Ḥanbal. They are called the *Mujtahid Imāms*, a rank that very few Muslims have ever reached. Most Muslims practice *Islām* by following the interpretations of these *Mujtahid Imāms*. All four of these schools of jurisprudence are recognized as authentic in *Islām*, and as each of their founders had the greatest respect and love for each other.

## Imām Abū Ḥanīfah

Abū Ḥanīfah was born in Basrah, Iraq in 80 A.H. (699 A.C.) He grew up and lived in Kufah, where he worked as a trader in textiles and also studied under famous scholars. He was a very gifted and intelligent student. He also traveled to Madinah to gain further knowledge.

He later became the greatest authority on religious jurisprudence (*Fiqh*) in Kufah, Iraq, and students from all over the Muslim world

220

came to study under his guidance.

Abū Hanīfah was very popular with the common people, who loved him for kindness and honesty in business. As a result, the rulers tried to win his favor, but he kept away from them, because they were unjust and often cruel.

When he was very old, the *Khalīfah* Al-Mansūr invited him to come to Baghdad as Chief Judge. Abū Hanīfah refused and replied: "Suppose a complaint is made against you in my court. You would want it to be decided in your favor, or have me thrown in the river. Please rest assured, I would prefer to be drowned in the river rather than tamper with justice."

Several *Khulafā'* and governors tried to make him work for their governments so that they could control him, but he refused despite persecution.

At last, the *Khalīfah* threw Abū Hanīfah into prison, where he died, at the age of 70. All the people of Baghdad mourned his death. Fifty thousand people attended his funeral prayers, which were offered for 20 days after his burial.

Abū Hanīfah is still famous today as the founder of one of the four schools of *Fiqh*. The Hanafi School is the largest in the world, and is followed by most people in the eastern and northern regions of the Muslim world including Turkey, the Balkans, Afghanistan, Pakistan, India, China, Central Asia and lower Egypt.

# Imām Mālik

Imām Mālik ibn Anas was born in Madinah in 93 A.H. (713 A.C.) He spent most of his life there. He studied under many teachers, many of whom were the students of *Ṣahābah* ﷺ. Imām Mālik chose to live in poverty and refused to be corrupted by riches.

Imām Mālik soon became famous as one of the most learned teachers of his time. When Imām Abū Hanīfah visited Madinah, he came to attend a lecture by Imām Mālik, even though Imām Mālik was 13 years younger than he was. Out of respect, Imām Mālik offered him his chair as the teacher.

Like Imām Abū Hanīfah, he had no fear of the *Khalīfah* Al-Mansūr or any other tyrannical ruler. He once openly defied the Governor of Madinah who was a cousin of the *Khalīfah*. The Imām told the people that their oath of loyalty to the *Khalīfah* was not binding since it had been given under threat of force. Despite warnings from the governor of Madinah, he persisted in opposing the injustice. Subsequently, the governor ordered him to be given 70 lashes, and then paraded him through the streets on a camel in his bloodstained clothes. Still, the Imām did not change his words. When *Khalīfah* AlMansūr got news of the incident, he punished the governor and apologized to the Imām.

Imām Mālik was so famous that when the *Khalīfah* Hārūn ﷺ ar-Rashid visited Madinah, he sent for the Imām to come and teach him. But the Imām insisted that the *Khalīfah* should come to him, saying: "People come in search of knowledge. Knowledge does not seek people." Eventually, the *Khalīfah* came to the Imām to hear his lectures. All classes of people attended them. The *Khalīfah* wanted the other people to be sent away, but the Imām refused, saying:

"I cannot sacrifice the interest of any individual for that of another." So, the *Khalīfah* and his sons had to submit to the Imām 's decision.

Imām Mālik wrote a number of famous books, dealing with all aspects of religious practice, law and ethics. One of the most well known is al-Muwaṭṭa, a collection of *Hadīth*.

Imām Mālik died at the age of 85. His school of *Fiqh*, known as the Maliki School, is now followed in most of Africa, except the extreme east of Africa and lower Egypt.


## Imām Ash-Shāfiʿī

Imām Muhammad ibn Idrīs Ash-Shāfiʿī was born in Palestine 150 years after the *Hijrah* (767 A.C.). His father died while he was young, and he was brought up in poverty by his mother.

Imām Ash-Shāfiʿī completed learning the Qur'ān by heart in Makkah. At the age of 20, he went to Madinah to study under Imām Mālik. He remained there until Imām Mālik's death, about eleven years later.

Imām Ash-Shāfiʿī spent part of his life in Iraq and then settled in Egypt. His entire life was spent in worship, writing and teaching.

He died at the age of 54 in Cairo. His school of *Fiqh* became very popular in the 3rd and 4th centuries AH. Today, its followers are found in many parts of the Muslim world, including Arabia, Palestine, Lebanon, Egypt, Malaysia, Indonesia and East Africa.

# Imām Aḥmad Ibn Hanbal

Imām Aḥmad ibn Hanbal was born in Iraq in 164 A.H. (780 A.C.) and grew up in Baghdad. His father died when he was about three years old. He studied *Fiqh* and *Ḥadīth* and other branches of religious knowledge. He traveled to various parts of the Muslim world to further his studies of *Ḥadīth*.

When Imām Ash-Shāfiʻī visited Baghdad, Imām Aḥmad studied under him. Imām Ash-Shāfiʻī considered him the most learned man in Baghdad. He became a well known teacher, and two of his pupils were al Bukhari and Muslim, who became famous for their collections of *Ḥadīth*.

He was at one time beaten and imprisoned for several years for opposing the views of the *Khalifah* on a matter of religious doctrine. However, he was so popular with the people as a learned and honest religious scholar that when he died at the age of 75, his funeral was attended by almost a million mourners in Baghdad.

Imām Aḥmad's pupils collected his answers to religious questions and systematized them into the form of the fourth school of *Fiqh*, known as the Ḥanbalī School. The true followers of this school of jurisprudence used to be found in Syria and Iraq, although it is scarcely in existence today.

# LESSON 7

---

## SOME NOTEWORTHY NIGERIAN MUSLIMS

### Shehu 'Uthmān Dan Fodio

Shehu 'Uthmān Dan Fodio was born in 1754 C.E. at Maratta, now known as the Niger Republic. He came from a family of learned Fulani Muslims and studied the Qur'ān under famous scholars. When he was 21, and still a student, he started teaching and preaching. His younger brother, Abdullahi, joined him as a student.

Both Shehu Uthmān and Abdullahi became famous scholars. They wrote books about Islām in Arabic and Fulfulde, a regional language. Shehu Uthman ﷺ called his people to follow the true teachings of Islām, and also called on the rulers not to inflict injustices on their people, but to rule in accordance with the *Sharī'ah*.

His son, Muhammad Bello, wrote of him: "He surpassed all men in nobility of character. He was a charming friend. He was generous and truthful. He was modest. He showed them a smiling face and was kind and happy to be with them. He was patient and had pity on Muslims."

Shehu Uthmān and his family settled in Degel in Gobir, near present-day Sokoto, Nigeria, and a community of scholars formed around him. Students and visitors wanted to learn the teachings of Islām from him.

The Shehu and his community called on their people to act in a righteous manner and abandon drinking alcohol. He called on the Muslim rulers to rule in accordance with the *Sharī'ah*, collect taxes lawfully and not imprison people illegally. He told the people of their rights under the *Sharī'ah* and advised them to appeal to the *Qadi* in the courts, if they did not get their due rights. He advised the rulers to appoint learned and fearless judges, on long preaching tours. Since they could not travel personally to all places, he wrote short books and poems that were translated into the regional languages. For those who could not read, songs were composed, teaching religion, known as *Wa'azi* songs.

After some years, when the Shehu's fame had spread far and wide in the surrounding areas, a new ruler of Gobir became jealous of the Shehu's influence. He made new laws forbidding people to change from paganism to *Islām* and forbidding Shehu's followers from preaching. The true Muslims began to leave Gobir.

The new ruler of Gobir died soon afterwards, but his son, Yunfa, continued his father's persecution of the Muslims, even seeking to kill Shehu Uthmān one occasion.

At last, open hostility broke out between the Chief of Gobir and the Shehu's community. The Chief sent a message to Shehu 'Uthmān, insisting that he take his family and leave his community. The Shehu replied: "I will not leave the community, but I will leave your country. Allāh's earth is widespread." Thus began the Shehu's *Hijrah* (migration).

The Shehu, his family, and the whole community then packed all their books and belongings on their cattle, horses, and camels, together with the little grain they had, and in February 1804, they began their trek out of Gobir.

They settled in Gudu, in Kebe, about 60 miles away, and the other Muslims in Gobir joined the Shehu to escape the persecutions of the Chief of Gobir.

The Gobirawa attacked the travelers and their families and robbed them of all their possessions.

The Chief of Gobir then declared war on the Shehu and his community The Muslims gave their promise of obedience to Shehu 'U<u>th</u>mān as *"Sarkin Musulmi,"* or "Commander of the Faithful," and began to prepare the defenses of the town for *Jihād*.

They were in a difficult situation. The Gobirawa had many fighters, horses and weapons. The Muslims had only about 20 horses, no shields and no heavy weapons. They relied chiefly on their bows and arrows.

Mallam Abdullahi led the army out of Gudu and caught the Gobir army by surprise near Lake Tabkin Kwatto. A battle was fought, and despite their greater numbers and equipment, the Gobir army was defeated. Therein followed a series of battles as each side increased its numbers with new recruits, and the Muslims lost many men in battle.

In 1805, the Gobir army attacked the Shehu's army just outside Gwandu. The Shehu went out and preached to his people. He prayed for victory and inspired the people to fight with all their might. The Gobirawa were defeated, and the tide of the war was turned.

From then on, the Shehu's followers, under the leadership of Mallam Abdullahi and the Shehu's son, Muhammad Bello, and later, other flag-bearers went from victory to victory, until all of Hausaland came under their rule, and some of the areas beyond it.

Shehu 'Uthmān finally settled in Sokoto, where he continued his studies and writing, and gave directives on government to his followers, until his death in 1817 C.E. All of his family was famous for scholarship, including his daughter, Asmau, who was a writer and poet.

Shehu 'Uthmān was without doubt the greatest Muslim scholar and reformer in Nigerian history. The books, in which he preached reform, purification of the religion from pagan practices and the supremacy of the law *(Sharī'ah)* are still read today. The Shehu's only intention was to preach in peace and persuade people to do right. It was the jealousy of the power-hungry rulers, such as Yunfa, which gave the Shehu no choice but to fight and defend themselves, and by the Grace of Allāh ﷻ, they succeeded.

Shehu 'Uthmān had many qualities that made him a successful leader. Firstly, his scholarship enabled him to perceive the difference between truth and falsehood, between the true social teachings of Islām and the non-Islāmic customs that the rulers and some of the people were practicing. Second, his care for the welfare of the common people, and his readiness to suffer discomfort in order to enlighten them about Islām and about their duties and rights as Muslims; he devoted his entire life to this cause. Lastly, one must admire his faith, steadfastness and courage in refusing to abandon his mission and in standing firm against the military power of the oppressors.

## Malam Abdullahi Dan Fodio

Malam Abdullahi was born in the Hausa State of Gobir around 1766-1767 C.E. He was 12 years younger than his brother, Shehu 'Uthmān.

He was taught the Qur'ān by his father, and when he had completed it's reading, he was taught by 'Uthmān and other scholars. He had a clear understanding of Islām and became a scholar and poet. He wrote many important books, and joined Shehu 'Uthmān in preaching reform among the Muslims.

When the time for *Jihād* came, Abdullahi became one of its most important leaders. In battle, Malam Abdullahi was very brave, setting an example to his followers, even when he was wounded. He could be firm and bold when necessary, but he was forgiving and generous in victory.

Malam Abdullahi was a very good Muslim. He did not seek wealth and pleasure but lived in a simple way, molding his life to the example of Rasūlullāh ﷺ .

He was very kind and merciful, especially towards the average person. He advised the rulers to treat them gently and not to demand too much of them. But he expected the educated leaders to have a strict code of conduct themselves. They had knowledge and power, and should therefore set the highest moral standards for others to emulate.

Malam Abdullahi's writing, preaching and example helped to spread the true teachings of *Islām* among the people.

When Shehu 'Uthmān withdrew from fighting in order to pursue his studies and writing, Malam Abdullahi was put in command of the western part of the territory. He was based in Gwandu, where he died in 1829 C.E. at the age of 66.

Shehu 'Uthmān and Malam Abdullahi were great scholars, sincere and truthful preachers, wise leaders, brave fighters and Muslims of high moral standards, famous not only throughout West Africa but also in other parts of the Muslim World.

## Muhammad El-Amin El-Kanemi

Muhammad El-Amin El-Kanemi was born in 1778 in a semi-desert region of Borno, north of Lake Chad. His father was Sheikh Langa of the Kanembu tribe and his mother was an Arab from North Africa. He was sent to school in Egypt and proved to be intelligent and having leadership qualities.

Upon completion of his studies, he accompanied his father to Makkah to perform the pilgrimage. They remained in Makkah for some years. His father fell ill and died at Madinah on their way home. El-Kanemi traveled on through Cairo to Tripoli in North Africa, where he stayed for some time to further his Qur'anic studies at the Kairouwan Mosque.

At last, he crossed the desert and reached home in Borno. The ruler of Borno was known as the Mai. The Mai appointed El-Kanemi as Chief of the Kanembu tribe. Because of his broad-based education, he became not only a chief but also an advisor and teacher among his people. He established his own school at Diffu, his base, and branches of the school in the surrounding areas staffed by his pupils. In this way, he developed a large following of scholars and pupils in Borno among the Kanembu, the Shua Arab and the Tubu tribes.

El-Kanemi was very concerned for the welfare of his people, and was strict in enforcing the *Sharī'ah*.

In 1804 C.E., a *Jihād* broke out in Kebbe and soon spread to other Hausa states under the leadership of Shehu 'Uthmān Dan Fodio. The

Fulanis (another tribe), in particular, joined the *Jihād*, and those settled in Borno rose against the Mai of Borno and captured his capital Ngazaramu.

The Mai fled and called on El-Kanemi and his large following to help him. El-Kanemi did not think much of the Mai because he was a weak leader, but he did not want to see Borno conquered by outsiders, so he gathered and trained a small army. He also wrote to Shehu Uthmān Dan Fodio and other local Fulani leaders, complaining about the attacks by Fulanis on fellow Muslims.

El-Kanemi drove the Fulanis out of Ngazargamu and restore the Mai to power. However, when he had returned to his home area, the Fulanis again drove out the Mai, and El-Kanemi led his men to defeat them once more.

El-Kanemi became a hero, and from that time, the Mais of Borno came to depend on him for protection. On El-Kanemi's advice, the Mai moved his capital further east to Birnin Kabela. At the request of the Mai, El-Kanemi established his own headquarters about 12 kilometers away. The method by which he selected its site is interesting. He and his followers set off on their horses reciting the Qur'ān, and they established their new headquarters at the spot where they completed the recitation of the entire Qur'ān.

There, El-Kanemi set up another school in his house. It is recorded that every night, between about 7:00 and 10:00 p.m., the Qur'ān would be read through 1,000 times in his house, which gives an idea of the incredible number of scholars who must have participated. Every Friday, before 'Asr prayer, they would read the Qur'an. Many people came to visit El-Kanemi and learn from him. Some built houses near his home, so that his settlement soon grew into a town, and was called Kukawa, after a Kuka tree that grew near his house. A special quarter of the town was set aside for Berber and Arab traders from North Africa, who also served as teachers in the school.

El-Kanemi became known as the Shehu of Borno, and he was so popular and powerful that he was able to depose any Mai whom he suspected of disloyalty to him and to appoint another member of the royal family to replace him.

Mai Dunama became jealous of El-Kanemi. He made a plot, along with another tribe, the Baghirmi, to attack and kill El-Kanemi. The plot was discovered by El-Kanemi, who turned the tables on the Mai. Instead, the Mai was killed himself by his own allies, and his capital was overrun by them. Meanwhile, El-Kanemi escaped.

The Baghirmi went home, leaving Borno without a Mai. The younger brother of Dunama, Ibrāhīm, promised to leave the real power to El-Kanemi if he could only bear the title of Mai. As a ruler, El-Kanemi proved to be very effective. He encouraged the Muslims to learn more about Islām and follow it correctly. He also maintained law and order throughout Borno.

The British traveler and explorer, Clapperton, visited Borno in 1822 and wrote of El-Kanemi: "No one could have used greater endeavors to substitute laws of reason for practices of barbarity and although feared, he is loved and respected. Compared to all around him, he is an angel and has subdued more by his generosity, mildness and benevolent disposition than by force of arms."

El-Kanemi fought other battles before his death, and due to his steadfastness, the Fulanis were never able to extend their rule to Borno.

El-Kanemi died in 1835 C.E., and was succeeded as Shehu by his son, 'Umar. He left behind him some of his written works, including a Tafsir of the Qur'ān, which is kept in Konduga today, and other books on *Tawḥīd*. He also left behind a great tradition of Islāmic scholarship in Borno, existing even today.

# IQRA' TRANSLITERATION CHART

| | | | | | |
|---|---|---|---|---|---|
| q | ق | * | z | ز | , | أء | * |
| k | ك | | s | س | | b | ب |
| l | ل | | <u>sh</u> | ش | | t | ت |
| m | م | | ṣ | ص | * | <u>th</u> | ث | * |
| n | ن | | ḍ | ض | * | j | ج |
| h | هـ | | ṭ | ط | * | ḥ | ح | * |
| w | و | | ẓ | ظ | * | <u>kh</u> | خ | * |
| y | ي | | ، | ع | | d | د | * |
| | | <u>gh</u> | غ | * | <u>dh</u> | ذ | * |
| | | f | ف | | r | ر |

| SHORT VOWELS | LONG VOWELS | DIPHTHONGS |
|---|---|---|
| a \ ـَ | a \ ـَا | aw \ ـَوْ |
| u \ ـُ | u \ ـُو | ai \ ـَيْ |
| i \ ـِ | i \ ـِي | |

| | | |
|---|---|---|
| Such as: *kataba* كَتَبَ | Such as: *Kitab* كِتَاب | Such as: *Lawḥ* لَوْح |
| Such as: *Qul* قُلْ | Such as: *Mamnun* مَمْنُون | Such as: *'Ain* عَيْن |
| Such as: *Ni'mah* نِعْمَة | Such as: *Dīn* دِين | |

\* Special attention should be given to the symbols marked with stars for they have no equivalent in the English sounds .

# ISLAMIC INVOCATIONS:

Rasūlullāh, *Ṣalla Allahu 'alaihi wa Sallam* ( صَلَّى ٱللّٰهُ عَلَيْهِ وَسَلَّم ), and the Qur'ān teaches us to glorify Allāh ﷻ when we mention His Name and to invoke His Blessings when we mention the names of His Angels, Messengers, the *Ṣaḥābah* and the Pious Ancestors.

When we mention the Name of Allāh we must say: *Subḥāna-hū Wa-Ta'ālā* ( سُبْحَانَهُ وَتَعَالَى ), Glorified is He and High. In this book we write an ﷻ to remind us to Glorify Allāh.

When we mention the name of Rasūlullāh ﷺ we must say: *Ṣalla Allāhu 'alai-hi wa-Sallam,* (صَلَّى ٱللّٰهُ عَلَيْهِ وَسَلَّم), May Allāh's Blessings and Peace be upon him.
We write an ﷺ to remind us to invoke Allāh's Blessings on Rasūlullāh.

When we mention the name of an angel or a prophet we must say: *Alai-hi-(a)s-Salām* (عَلَيْهِ ٱلسَّلاَم), Upon him be peace.
We write an ؑ to remind us to invoke Allāh's Peace upon him.

When we hear the name of the *Ṣaḥābah* we must say:
For more than two, *Raḍiya-(A)llāhu Ta'ālā 'an-hum,* (رَضِيَ ٱللّٰهُ تَعَالَى عَنْهُم), May Allāh be pleased with them.
For two of them, *Raḍiya-(A)llāhu Ta'ālā 'an-humā* ( رَضِيَ ٱللّٰهُ تَعَالَى عَنْهُمَا ), May Allāh be pleased with both of them.
For a *Ṣaḥābī, Raḍiya-(A)llāhu Ta'ālā 'an-hu* ( رَضِيَ ٱللّٰهُ تَعَالَى عَنْهُ ), May Allāh be pleased with him.
For a *Ṣaḥābiyyah, Raḍiya-(A)llāhu Ta'ālā 'an-hā* ( رَضِيَ ٱللّٰهُ تَعَالَى عَنْهَا ), May Allāh be pleased with her.
We write an ؓ to remind us to invoke Allāh's Pleasure with a *Ṣaḥābī,* a *Sahabiyah* or with *Ṣaḥābah.*

When we hear the name of the Pious Ancestor *(As-Salaf as-Ṣāliḥ)* we must say.
For a man, *Raḥmatu-(A)llāh 'alai-hi* (رَحْمَةُ ٱللّٰهِ عَلَيْهِ), May Allāh's Mercy be upon him.
For a woman, *Raḥmatu-(A)llāh 'alai-hā* ( رَحْمَةُ ٱللّٰهِ عَلَيْهَا ), May Allāh's Mercy be with her.

# ABOUT THE AUTHOR

B. Aisha Lemu is of British origin. She accepted Islām in 1961. She was Principal of the Government Girls College, Sokoto, Nigeria, from 1968-1976 and Principal of the Women Teachers College, Mina from 1976-1977. In addition to teaching Islāmic Studies for several years, she has written numerous books and articles on Islāmic topics. The revised edition of her other famous textbook, *Tawhid and Fiqh*, is being published by IQRA' Foundation concurrently. She is now Director of the Islāmic Education Trust, Mina, Nigeria and is world-renowned in the field of Islāmic education in Africa and Islāmic world